ANCIENT
ART OF THE

AMERICAN
WOODLAND
INDIANS

ANCIENT ART OF THE
AMERICAN WOODLAND INDIANS

Text by David S. Brose,
James A. Brown, and
David W. Penney

Photographs by Dirk Bakker

Harry N. Abrams, Inc., Publishers, New York
in association with the Detroit Institute of Arts

Front cover: Hand-Shaped Cutout, Middle Woodland period, 200 B.C.–A.D. 400 (cat. no. 28)

Back cover: (top) Panther-Effigy Pipe, Middle Woodland period, A.D. 1–400 (cat no. 55); (bottom) Double Bottle (Hudson Engraved), Late Mississippian period, A.D. 1500–1800 (cat. no. 71)

Half-title page: Locust-Shaped Bead, Late Archaic period, 1500–700 B.C. (cat. no. 17)

Frontispiece: Engraved Shell Gorget Showing Two Bird-Men, Late Mississippian period, A.D. 1300–1500 (cat. no. 124)

Project Director: Michael Kan
Organizing Curator and Catalogue Coordinator: David W. Penney
Editor: Andrea P. A. Belloli
Designer: Darilyn Lowe

Library of Congress Cataloging in Publication Data

Brose, David S.
 Ancient art of the American Woodland Indians.

 Catalogue of a traveling exhibition to be held at the National Gallery of Art, Washington, D.C., the Detroit Institute of Arts, and the Houston Museum of Fine Arts, Mar. 17, 1985-Mar. 2, 1986.
 Bibliography: p.
 1. Woodland Indians—Art—Exhibitions. 2. Indians of North America—Art—Exhibitions. I. Brown, James Allison, 1934-   . II. Penney, David W. III. Bakker, Dirk. IV. Detroit Institute of Arts. V. National Gallery of Art (U.S.) VI. Museum of Fine Arts, Houston. VII. Title.
 E78,E2B76 1985   730',O974'O74O13   84-20462
 ISBN 0-8109-1827-7
 ISBN 0-89558-105-1 (Detroit Institute of Arts: pbk.)

Printed and bound in Japan

CONTENTS

This catalogue is published in conjunction with the exhibition
"Ancient Art of the American Woodland Indians,"
which has been made possible by generous grants from

The National Endowment for the Arts, a Federal agency
The Stroh Foundation
Founders Society Detroit Institute of Arts

The Alexander Collection, Epps, Louisiana

The Brooklyn Museum

Center for American Archeology, Kampsville, Illinois

The Dennis Labatt Collection, Epps, Louisiana

The Detroit Institute of Arts

Etowah Mounds Archaeological Area [Cartersville] and Kolo-
    moki Mounds Museum [Blakely], Parks and Historic Sites
    Division, Georgia Department of Natural Resources, Atlanta

Florida State Museum, Gainesville

Frank H. McClung Museum, University of Tennessee, Knoxville

The Gordon Hart Collection, Bluffton, Indiana

The Guennol Collection, Brooklyn, New York

Illinois Archaeological Survey, Urbana

Illinois Department of Transportation, Springfield

Illinois State Museum of Natural History and Art, Springfield

The Mound City Group National Monument, National Parks
    Service, Chillicothe, Ohio

The Museum of the American Indian, Heye Foundation,
    New York, New York

The National Museum of Natural History, Smithsonian
    Institution, Washington, D.C.

Ohio Historical Society, Columbus

Peabody Museum of Archaeology and Ethnology, Harvard
    University, Cambridge, Massachusetts

Robert S. Peabody Foundation for Archaeology, Phillips
    Academy, Andover, Massachusetts

St. Louis Museum of Science and Natural History

Southern Illinois University, Center for Archaeological
    Investigations, Carbondale

Temple Mound Museum, Fort Walton Beach, Florida

Thomas Gilcrease Institute of American History and Art, Tulsa,
    Oklahoma

University of Alabama Museum of Natural History, University

University of Arkansas Museum, Fayetteville

University of Georgia, Department of Anthropology, Athens

University of Illinois Museum of Natural History, Urbana

University of Michigan Museum of Anthropology, Ann Arbor

Washington University Gallery of Art, St. Louis

PREFACE AND ACKNOWLEDGMENTS

As early as the eighteenth century in the United States of America, the study of Native American prehistoric art was deemed an important area of art historical and archaeological research. Institutions such as the American Philosophical Society, founded by Benjamin Franklin in 1743, Peale's Museum, founded in 1786 (later known as the Philadelphia Museum), and New England's American Antiquarian Society, founded in 1812, were devoted to the study, collection, and preservation of the antiquities of North America. In the 1840s, under the aegis of the American Ethnological Society, G. E. Squier and E. H. Davis pioneered the research of mounds in the eastern United States in an effort to determine whether they were part of the ancient heritage of Native Americans or remnants of another, lost civilization (their findings were published in *Ancient Monuments of the Mississippi Valley* in 1848 by the newly founded Smithsonian Institution).

During the span of time from the second half of the nineteenth century through the first three decades of the twentieth century, however, New World archaeology in the United States developed as an academic discipline classified with anthropology and the social sciences and separated from art history and the humanities. Paradoxically, given the early interest in the art of prehistoric North America and the fact that Classical, or Old World, archaeology traditionally spawned archaeologists who were equally active as art historians, New World archaeology was not accepted as a part of art history.

A resurgence of recognition and general public awareness of Native American art began in the 1930s and early 1940s. Laurence V. Coleman, in *The Museum in America* (Washington, D.C., 1939:83), stated that "The most conspicuous gap among the arts has been left by giving aboriginal art of the New World to the Anthropologists." In an effort to lessen this gap, such exhibitions as the 1931 "Exposition of Indian Tribal Arts," organized by John Sloan and Oliver La Farge, were mounted. The exposition was followed in 1939 by a major exhibition at the San Francisco World's Fair, organized by Frederic H. Douglas and René d'Harnoncourt, that ultimately developed into the 1941 show, "Indian Art of the United States," at the Museum of Modern Art, New

York (the exhibition was accompanied by a catalogue that has become a landmark in literature of the field). Due to the interest created by these exhibitions, existing collections of Native American art, such as that of the Metropolitan Museum of Art, New York, gained recognition and new collections, such as that of the Denver Art Museum, began to be formed.

Through further museum displays and the publications of Dr. Frederick J. Dockstader of the Museum of the American Indian, Heye Foundation, and Norman Feder, Curator at the Denver Art Museum, Native American art continued to gain acceptance in the 1950s through the early 1970s. As a result, in 1977 and 1978 two comprehensive exhibitions of high artistic merit, "Sacred Circles," organized by Ralph T. Coe, and "The Native American Heritage," organized by Dr. Evan M. Maurer, received wide acclaim.

It is particularly fitting that the exhibition "Ancient Art of the American Woodland Indians" has been organized by the Department of African, Oceanic, and New World Cultures of the Detroit Institute of Arts. In the short space of seven years since the department was first established in 1976, such major acquisitions as the 664-piece Chandler/Pohrt Collection of Great Lakes Indian Art have brought the Native American collections of the Detroit Institute of Arts into national prominence. It is hoped that this exhibition, which focuses specifically on the archaeological art of the American Woodland Indians, will encourage other scholars and art museums to further specialize in and develop studies of Native American art within the discipline of art history.

Michael Kan

The support and cooperation of many individuals and institutions have been crucial to the realization of "Ancient Art of the American Woodland Indians." Those who generously consented to lend priceless treasures to the exhibition are listed elsewhere in this volume; to them we offer our deepest gratitude. We also wish to thank the following individuals who, in their capacity as professionals representing the institutions with which they are associated, extended special assistance: Kenneth E. Apschnikat, Bradley Baker, Natasha Bonilla, Thomas Brayshaw, Rudy Busto, Jeffrey Chapman, Diana Fane, Ken Farnsworth, David Hally, Martha Hayes, Harry Henriksen, Michael and Peggy Hoffman, James G. Houser, Richard W. Jeffries, Joseph Ketner II, Dennis Labatt, Yulee Lazarus, Amos Lovejoy, Lea McChesney, Daniel McPike, Gerald Milanich, John O'Shea, Martha Potter Otto, Frank Schnell, Bruce D. Smith, James Smith, John Speth, Elizabeth Steiner, Bonnie Styles, Billy Townsend, John Walthall, Lee Warner, and

Deborah Woodiel. Several persons who shared their expertise in a variety of ways deserve special mention: Anna Roosevelt, Museum of the American Indian, Heye Foundation; Clarence H. Webb; Howard D. Winters, Professor of Anthropology, New York University; and Stuart Struever, Director, Center for American Archeology, who participated extensively in the initial planning stages of the exhibition and catalogue. At the National Gallery of Art, Gaillard Ravenel and Mark Leithauser were responsible for the design of the exhibition and Dodge Thompson was responsible for its administration. We extend our appreciation to them and to the numerous members of the staff of the Detroit Institute of Arts who lent their enthusiastic and able assistance to the creation of the exhibition and its catalogue.

A deep debt of gratitude goes to two of the catalogue authors, David S. Brose and James A. Brown, not only for their excellent essays, but also for generously making available their incomparable expertise during all phases of the exhibition's organization. Andrea P. A. Belloli, as catalogue editor, did an outstanding job under considerably less than perfect conditions. We are also grateful to Harry N. Abrams, Inc., New York, for their commitment to the exhibition and its catalogue and wish especially to mention Margaret L. Kaplan, Senior Vice-President and Executive Editor, who first expressed interest in the book and oversaw its development, and Joanne Greenspun, who lent editorial assistance and saw the catalogue through production. Darilyn Lowe brought a special sensitivity to the design of this publication. A final credit must go to David W. Penney, the organizing curator of the exhibition and the third catalogue author, who has nurtured this project into being over the last several years.

Michael Kan, Acting Director and Curator of African, Oceanic, and New World Cultures, The Detroit Institute of Arts
J. Carter Brown, Director, National Gallery of Art
Peter C. Marzio, Director, The Museum of Fine Arts, Houston

INTRODUCTION

David W. Penney

The Woodlands of North America stretch from the eastern edge of the Great Plains to the Atlantic seaboard, from Hudson Bay to the Gulf of Mexico. Heavily forested, riddled with lakes and rivers, broken on the east by the northeast-southwest sweep of the Appalachians, the Woodlands supported thousands of generations of inhabitants long before Europeans began to explore the world and stumbled upon the Americas. The Woodlands are rich in resources and have fostered the development of a number of strategies for living: from itinerant hunting and gathering to well-organized agriculture, from egalitarian bands to nearly totalitarian chiefdoms.

Archaeologists have attempted to recover the record of native Woodlands cultural history by carefully sifting through the remains of the past. The primary source for the archaeological historian is the artifact and its context—a tool discarded in a midden, or rubbish heap, for example—that reveals, through its association with other tools and materials, when it was made, what it was used for, and how it fit into an overall plan for living. While most artifacts recovered by archaeologists reflect day-to-day concerns, some reveal that special attention was paid to the techniques of their manufacture and to their decoration. These objects often appear to have been intended to convey special information regarding the status of their owners or, in some cases, the cosmological world view of an entire society. The archaeological record of the Woodlands is rich in such art works, which reveal a complex and comprehensive iconographic tradition. Thus the great masterworks from the eastern United States inform us both about the manner in which Woodlands peoples conceptualized the world they lived in and the ways in which they organized their lives.

A basic chronology for cultural development in the eastern Woodlands was established nearly fifty years ago when Gordon R. Willey and James A. Ford (1941) proposed a sequence from the Archaic through the Burial Mound to the Temple Mound period. Later this sequence was refined by James B. Griffin to embrace the terms Paleo-Indian (12,000–8000 B.C.), Archaic (8000–1000 B.C.), Woodland (1000 B.C.–A.D. 1000), and Mississippian (A.D. 1000–1600), although the premises for the period divisions remained the same. Each was considered a discreet cultural stage. "Paleo-Indian" referred to a free-wandering lifestyle focused on big-game hunting. The Archaic was based on the concept of a hunting and gathering economy without pottery. People of the Woodland period were considered agriculturists for whom the chiefdom was the characteristic form of social organization. Finally, Mississippian societies were believed to have developed an incipient stage of civilization comparable to the cultures of Mesoamerica. The Archaic, Woodland, and Mississippian were further subdivided into early, middle, and late sub-periods (Griffin 1952c).

Research since mid-century has proven that some of these assumptions were false. Woodland-period peoples were not agriculturists, although they were aware of some domesticated plants. The Late Archaic had much more in common with the Early Woodland than with the Middle Archaic. The Late Woodland period is better understood as the beginning of the Mississippian phase than as the end of the Woodland period. Mississippian societies developed into complex chiefdoms, but did not approach the level of social organization exhibited by the civilizations of Mesoamerica. Nevertheless the terminology and dating sequence for these major divisions has endured and has been adopted for *Ancient Art of the American Woodland Indians*. Recent qualifications to this chronological system are discussed in the various essays.

This art historical survey of the eastern Woodlands begins with the Late Archaic period because the cultural patterns and institutions that resulted in the emergence of an indigenous North American art tradition began to develop during that time. These same patterns and institutions continued to provide the impetus for the making of art through the Middle Woodland period. The Late Archaic, Early Woodland, and Middle Woodland periods thus comprise the first major phase of North American art history. Agriculture, which provided the basis for the next period of cultural growth, the Mississippian, resulted in a major reorganization of Woodlands cultural systems. The less flexible structures of Mississippian social hierarchy and religious belief are evident in art of that era.

Since an accurate picture of Woodlands prehistory is just beginning to emerge, the history of art in that area remains in a fledgling stage as well. For this reason, each of the first three essays in *Ancient Art of the American Woodland Indians* discusses one of the traditional chronological divisions. These essays describe the numerous local cultural traditions and their interrelationships and sequences, providing a basis for an understanding of Woodlands society and art. The final essay attempts to identify and interpret the basic themes of Woodlands art and how these were elaborated over some five thousand years of prehistory. It is our hope that this volume—and the exhibition it documents, the first of its kind—will provide a foundation for the understanding of a long-neglected topic of national importance: the cultural and artistic history of the first inhabitants of the North American Woodlands.

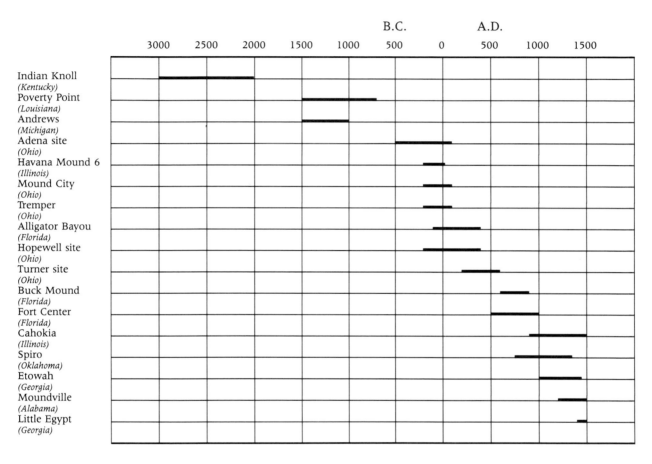

Timeline for Woodlands region sites

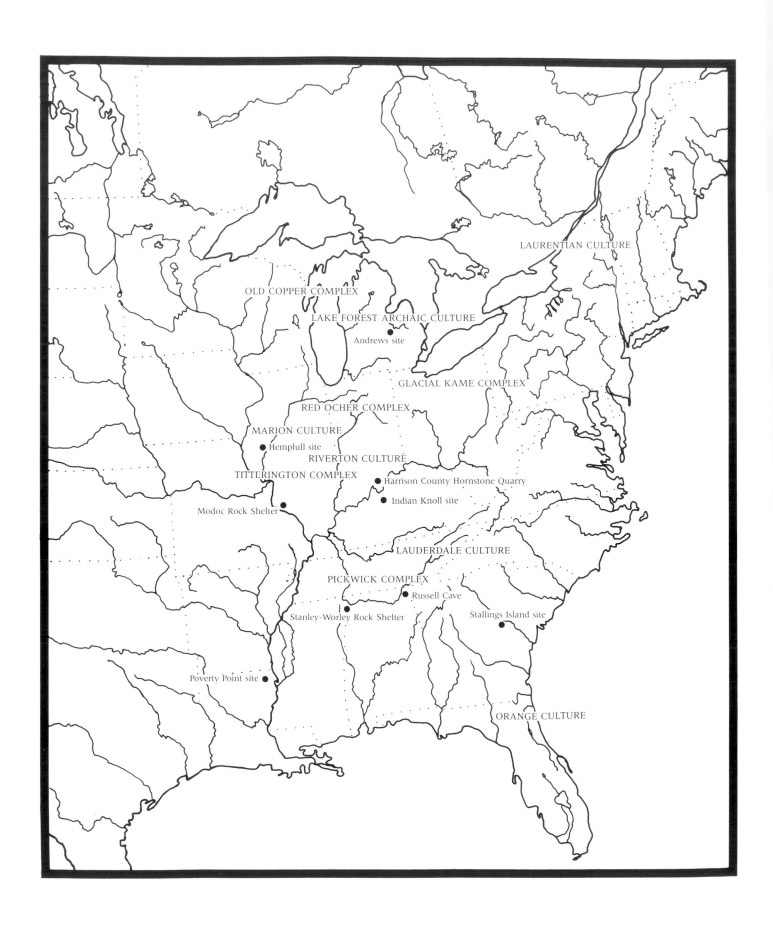

LAURENTIAN CULTURE

OLD COPPER COMPLEX

LAKE FOREST ARCHAIC CULTURE
● Andrews site

GLACIAL KAME COMPLEX

RED OCHER COMPLEX

MARION CULTURE
● Hemplull site
RIVERTON CULTURE
TITTERINGTON COMPLEX
● Harrison County Hornstone Quarry
● Indian Knoll site
Modoc Rock Shelter ●

LAUDERDALE CULTURE

PICKWICK COMPLEX
● Russell Cave
Stanley-Worley Rock Shelter ●
Stallings Island site
●

Poverty Point site ●

ORANGE CULTURE

I. THE LATE ARCHAIC PERIOD*

David W. Penney

The Archaic Period

The notion of an Archaic period of Woodlands history is intended to describe a pattern of gradual adaptation of New World peoples to a number of diverse ecological systems and geographic terrains following the era of more general big-game hunting referred to as the Paleo-Indian period (12,000–8000 B.C.). The earliest known Native American peoples hunted now-extinct species of bison, tapir, ground sloth, camel, and mammoth. Paleo-Indian sites, generally confined to the plains and prairies of North America, characteristically are "kill-sites"—consisting of the butchered remains of hunted animals with associated tools and debris—rather than habitations. After 8000 B.C. the archaeological record reveals a movement of population into regions with a greater variety of ecological conditions and adaptations to locally available resources. There is a sharp discontinuity between the weapon and tool types of the Paleo-Indian and Early Archaic traditions. The succeeding cultural history of the Archaic period may be characterized as the development and elaboration of many different kinds of technologies in order to best utilize the resources of a given territory.

The Archaic encompassed some seven thousand years of cultural change, which can be divided into three sub-periods: the Early (8000–5000 B.C.), Middle (5000–3000 B.C.), and Late Archaic (3000–1000 B.C.). Although this sequence implies the beginning, middle, and end of a cultural epoch, this is a false impression. Research into the Late Archaic done after this chronology was initially proposed has shown that although the Early and Middle Archaic followed a relatively cohesive tendency of cultural development, the Late Archaic is best described as a period of innovation and change, a beginning rather than an ending.

Our understanding of the Early and Middle Archaic periods stems from a small number of successively occupied sites—pri-

Opposite:
Late Archaic period sites and culture areas

Overleaf:
Plate 1. Bannerstone, chalcedony, Indian Knoll culture, Late Archaic period, 3000–2000 B.C. (cat. no. 1.1).

Plate 2. Bannerstone, granite, Indian Knoll culture, Late Archaic period, 3000–2000 B.C. (cat. no. 1.2).

Plate 3. Bannerstone, chalcedony, Indian Knoll culture, Late Archaic period, 3000–2000 B.C. (cat. no. 1.3).

* The author wishes to thank and acknowledge Howard D. Winters and David S. Brose for their help and advice as well as for the use of some of their unpublished writings, all of which have been incorporated into this essay. However, any faults in interpretation or conclusions are his own.

16

Plate 4. Bannerstone, siliceous rock, Indian Knoll culture, Late Archaic period, 3000–2000 B.C. (cat. no. 1.4).

Plate 5. Bannerstone, banded clay stone, Indian Knoll culture, Late Archaic period, 3000–2000 B.C. (cat. no. 1.5).

marily caves and rock shelters such as the Modoc Rock Shelter in Illinois and the Stanford-Worley Bluff shelter and Russell Cave site, both in Alabama—where the chronological sequences of various Archaic-period artifact types could be established. These were compared to artifacts found in more isolated contexts throughout the Woodlands region. Certain projectile point styles, such as Dalton points, Kirk points, and several others, were distributed across vast territories, suggesting that the peoples who used them moved freely throughout a sparsely populated landscape. Different point types tend to conform to broad ecological zones, indicating some cultural diversity based on groups of people adapting to preferred geographic conditions.

In general, Early and Middle Archaic peoples sought out a wide variety of food sources, hunting big game, many kinds of smaller animals, and waterfowl and gathering many species of edible wild plants. Several technological innovations occurred during this time. *Manos* and *metates* (mortars and pestles) were used for processing plant foods. Woodworking tools such as axes, adzes, knives, drills, abraders, scrapers for hide-working, and awls and needles for sewing and basketmaking all testify to a rich material culture. By 5000 B.C. many of these fabricating and processing tools were being made from laboriously pecked and ground stone, rather than from chipped flints and cherts (flintlike rocks). Few items of adornment and no recognizable ceremonial equipment have been found dating prior to around 4000 B.C., although this may be due to a shortage of datable examples.

The Late Archaic Period

Late Archaic cultures continued to become more specialized in exploiting local ecological conditions. Relatively large settlements were established within many of the river valleys of central North America, and their cultural traditions began to exhibit strong regional characteristics. Concomitant with this definition of "ethnic boundaries" (Brose 1979b:6) was an increased concern with the social and political relationships within and between territorial groups. Evidence of warfare is not uncommon, indicating that neighboring communities with expanding populations were in competition for the most richly endowed locations. Another means of smoothing territorial frictions, amply illustrated in ethnological literature (Dalton 1977), was the creation and maintenance of trade relationships between groups. The reciprocal obligations of trade created possibilities for alliances, intermarriage, and the possibility of pooling resources in case of shortages in local food supplies. The procurement and exchange of various

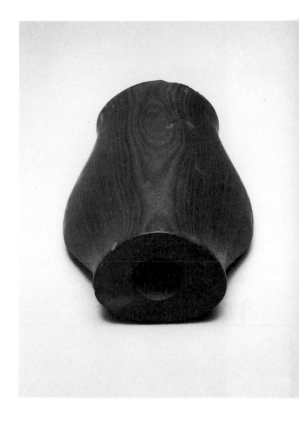

Plate 6. Bannerstone, banded clay stone, Indian Knoll culture, Late Archaic period, 3000–2000 B.C. (cat. no. 1.6).

Overleaf:
Plate 7. Bannerstone, banded slate, Late Archaic period, 2000–1000 B.C. (cat. no. 2).

Plate 8. Notched Ovate Bannerstone, banded slate, Late Archaic period, 2000–1000 B.C. (cat. no. 3).

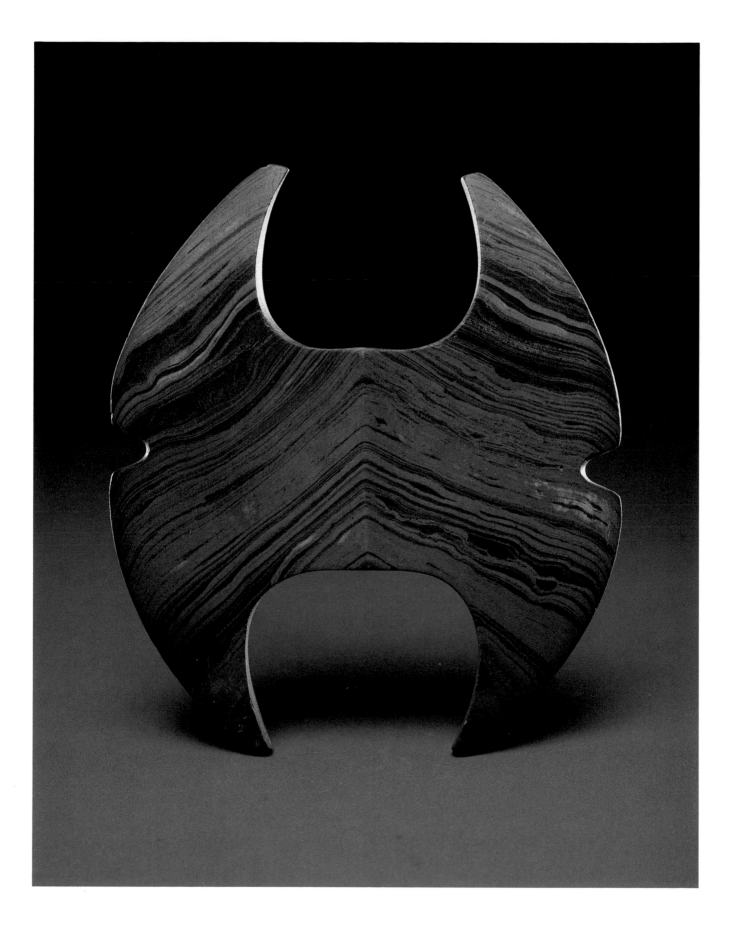

Plate 9. Butterfly-Shaped Bannerstone, banded slate, Late Archaic period, 3000–1000 B.C. (cat. no. 4).

Plate 10. Knobbed Lunate Bannerstone, banded slate, Late Archaic/Early Woodland period, 1000–500 B.C. (cat. no. 5).

Plate 11. Oval Bannerstone, sandstone, Lauderdale culture, Late Archaic period, 2000–1000 B.C. (cat. no. 6).

Plate 12. Bannerstone, porphyry, Titterington complex, Late Archaic period, 1500–500 B.C. (cat. no. 7).

kinds of economically valuable and symbolic substances became an important mechanism for political interaction between groups during the Late Archaic.

Several regional trade networks can be discerned during this period. Copper (pls. 13–15) circulated widely throughout the Great Lakes and St. Lawrence drainage, but rarely appeared south of the Ohio River before the Woodland period (Fogel 1963). Various kinds of fine cherts, such as Harrison County hornstone from Indiana, circulated throughout the same region as well as the Midwest. Marine shell was transported in vast quantities into the southeastern interior and began to appear regularly in Great Lakes-region burials after about 1500 B.C. (pl. 21). Steatite, or soapstone, quarried from sources in the central Appalachians, was brought into the Northeast and throughout the South as far west as the Mississippi Delta. Galena (a soft lead-sulfide mineral), slate, jasper (pls. 23–28), and other precious stones also entered the Late Archaic trade networks. Patterns of dispersal suggest that other local networks existed, which combined into northern and southern patterns without a great deal of interaction between one pattern and the other until later in the Woodland period.

In the Midwest and Southeast, the Late Archaic subsistence base narrowed to a small number of heavily exploited food sources, as opposed to the typical Early and Middle Archaic pattern of a wide-spectrum economy. Among the most important of these were freshwater mussels. These had always been a source of nourishment for Archaic peoples, but they only became a major resource during the Late Archaic period—so much so that this stage of Late Archaic life has been termed the "shell-mound Archaic" after the large piles of mussel debris that characterize many Late Archaic riverside sites. The other significant food sources were deer and nuts. Remains of the latter have been noted only recently at Late Archaic sites as a result of modern flotation techniques, which permit the recovery of minute particles of nut shells, seeds, and other plant substances.

The shell-mound middens reflect a mere portion of the year's economic activity—shellfish gathering—which was accompanied by the non-intensive hunting and gathering of fresh, wild foods during the summer months. Later in the year, Late Archaic groups dispersed to nut-gathering locations along valley bluffs, moving finally to winter hunting camps in the highlands, only to return to riverside base camps the following summer. This kind of "central-based wandering," or seasonal round of hunting and gathering activity, characterizes the economies of several well-known historic-period Indian groups. Economic insurance developed from techniques for food storage in pits or transport in baskets. Food could thus be "banked" for future use. The narrow-spectrum

Plate 13. Socketed Blade, copper, Old Copper complex, Late Archaic period, 1500–500 B.C. (cat. no. 8.1).

Plate 14. Knife, copper, Old Copper complex, Late Archaic period, 1500–500 B.C. (cat. no. 8.2).

Plate 15. Serrated Tanged Blade and Crescent Knife, copper, Old Copper complex, Late Archaic period, 2000–1000 B.C. (cat. no. 9.1–.2).

economy, intensive use of local water sources, and methods of managing resources over time contributed to increased territorial stability and dramatic population growth (Winters 1974).

Changes in settlement patterns and subsistence strategies during the Late Archaic were accompanied by other significant innovations. Ceremonial equipment such as rattles, flutes, and smoking pipes first appeared during this period. Ornaments, pendants, and beads made of valuable, often imported materials were produced in unprecedented abundance (pls. 20–27). Mortuary ceremonialism became much more elaborate, involving delayed burial of ritually prepared remains, the sprinkling of the dead with red ocher pigment, and the equipping of burials with various kinds of offerings. All of these aspects of Late Archaic life established patterns visible in exaggerated form during the Woodland period.

One of the best-known and largest Late Archaic shell middens is the Indian Knoll site (3000–2000 B.C.) located on the banks of an extinct channel of the Green River in Kentucky. Nearly fifty-five thousand artifacts and more than a thousand burials were recovered from this site. Although post molds riddled the habitation areas, the structural character of the houses could not be determined from them. Burials of individuals flexed in near-fetal positions were interred in rounded pits, sometimes sprinkled with red ocher or equipped with burial offerings, then covered with midden debris. Grave goods included tools and weapons such as chipped flint blades or beautifully made bannerstones, or *atlatl* weights (pls. 1–6), discussed in detail below; ceremonial equipment (rattles and flutes) or beads; and pendants and other ornaments, often made of marine shell imported from the Atlantic coast or, more rarely, copper (Moore 1916; W. S. Webb 1946).

Similar riverine settlement systems include the Riverton culture (1500–1000 B.C.), located in the central Wabash valley of southern Illinois and Indiana (Winters 1969), and the Lauderdale culture (3500–1000 B.C.) of the Tennessee River valley (Lewis and Kneberg 1959; Walthall 1980:68–76). To the north, people of the Great Lakes Forest Archaic (Tuck 1978) established large, lakeside villages for seasonal fishing, but dispersed to midsummer gathering locations and winter hunting camps as small family units. Along the Atlantic coast, a similar pattern of large seasonal settlements close to seaside resources and small interior hunting and gathering camps also prevailed. The Stallings Island culture (3000–1000 B.C.) of the Savannah River valley in Georgia and South Carolina exhibited a typical Late Archaic focus on shellfish and deer, although a detailed understanding of Stallings Island economy remains in the future (Stoltman 1974). The earliest North American pottery, a coarse, undecorated ware tempered

Plate 16. Three Birdstones, granitic porphyry, slate (limonite stain), green Huronian slate, Red Ocher complex, Late Archaic period, 1500–1000 B.C. (cat. no. 10.1–.3).

with vegetable fibers, is associated with the Stallings Island culture and dates from as early as 2500 B.C. A similar fiber-tempered ware, known as Orange ware, appeared along the St. Johns and Indian rivers in Florida by 2000 B.C. Shoreline habitations were occupied nearly year-round on the coastal islands of the Carolinas, around the Florida peninsula, and among the sounds and bayous of the Gulf Coast from Tampa Bay to east Texas. These

societies fished, hunted sea mammals, and collected esturine mollusks.

A similar Archaic shellfish and hunting economy existed in the lower Mississippi Delta region between 3000 and 2000 B.C. Small fired-clay balls were employed for "stone cooking," a method typically used by many North American peoples, in which a heated stone is used to cook liquids in a vessel or in earth ovens. The marshy coastal plain was poor in raw materials for tool-making. Chert and other stones had to be imported from up-river sources, allowing settlements situated in strategic locations along the Mississippi valley to achieve a lucrative "middleman" status (Gibson 1980). One such settlement was Poverty Point, located on the Bayou Maçon in northeast Louisiana, which, by 1000 B.C., had grown to a sizable town with a population numbering some five thousand inhabitants.

Poverty Point was the largest and most complex Late Archaic site in North America. House structures were built on a series of six concentric embankments, thus forming an immense semicircle twelve hundred meters wide that opened onto the bluffs overlooking the Bayou Maçon. The embankments average six feet in height and are eighty feet across and one hundred fifty feet apart (**fig. 1**). Overlooking the settlement to the west is mound A, a large earthen mound some seventy feet high and 640 feet across, shaped like an enormous bird, oriented to the west with wings extended (**fig. 2**). Three other large mounds, called mound B, Motley, and Jackson, were constructed nearby. The purpose of the mounds, whether temple platforms or burial monuments, is not clear (Ford and Webb 1956).

Several other large sites and a series of smaller settlements located in Louisiana and Mississippi comprise the Poverty Point culture. The larger sites and their associated communities were linked together by a complex network of trade relationships, importing flints and cherts from the north, steatite from the Appalachians, and a variety of other valuable materials: galena, hematite (a mineral consisting chiefly of an oxide of iron), sandstone, jasper, slate, and so on (Gibson 1980). The Poverty Point site itself developed a sophisticated lapidary tradition for the manufacture of minute effigy pendants and beads of highly polished red jasper (**pls. 23–27**). The first known human figurines from North America, made from fired clay, also were found at the Poverty Point site (**pl. 30**). Many of these resemble pregnant females so that some sort of fertility association is possible.

The Poverty Point site, with its emphasis on trade and elaboration of luxury items for the mercantile elite, hints at the dramatic developments of the Middle Woodland period. Evidently these trade networks collapsed prematurely, however, since the site did not remain active after around 700 B.C.

Burial Complexes

During the latter part of the Late Archaic period (2000–1000 B.C.) burials were often located far from any settlement. The burial ceremony combined esoteric rites with special classes of objects as burial offerings that are often difficult to relate to patterns observed in occupation sites. As a result, the Late Archaic includes a number of mortuary "complexes," or groups of observed traits— such as preferred burial locations, ritual treatment of the dead, and distinctive kinds of artifacts—that cannot be assigned specifically to a recognized cultural system.

The Old Copper complex (3000–500 B.C.) consists of a number of burial sites and isolated discoveries of characteristic artifacts in Wisconsin, Upper Michigan, and Ontario, Canada. Its name comes from a series of distinctive copper tools, projectile points,

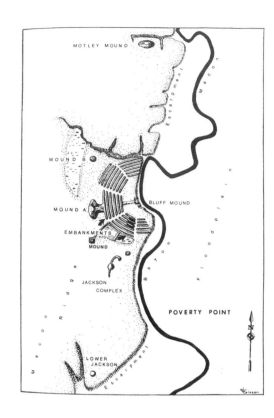

Figure 1. Plan of the Poverty Point site, West Carroll Parish, Louisiana. Reproduced from Gibson 1983:11, fig.4.

Figure 2. View of mound A, Poverty Point site, West Carroll Parish, Louisiana.

blades, knives, awls, and axes that typically accompany burials as grave offerings **(pls. 13–15)**. The copper was collected from several sources within the upper Great Lakes area—notably the Keewenaw Peninsula and Isle Royale—where large nuggets of nearly pure native copper can be quarried from easily accessible veins. The tools were hammered, cut, and annealed into shape without the benefit of casting or other more advanced metallurgical techniques. In light of their popularity as high-status burial offerings and their circulation within the Great Lakes area, the copper tools probably functioned as valued exchange items and objects of status rather than as strictly utilitarian implements. No western Great Lakes Old Copper settlements have been located. The copper tool assemblage resembles the ground slate tools of the eastern Laurentian tradition of New England, which is much better documented with a variety of sites (Tuck 1978). The Old Copper burial complex probably fits into the Great Lakes Forest Archaic as a specialized burial/exchange component of its cultural system.

The Titterington complex refers to a series of poorly dated sites distributed along the bluffs of the Illinois and Mississippi rivers in Illinois and Missouri. Typically a few individuals were interred with ground and polished bannerstones **(pl. 12)**, teardrop-shaped plummets, and caches of large, finely chipped flint or chert

Plate 17. Popeyed Birdstone, speckled porphyry, Red Ocher/ Glacial Kame complex, Late Archaic/Early Woodland period, 1500–500 B.C. (cat. no. 11).

Plate 18. Popeyed Birdstone, porphyry, Red Ocher/Glacial Kame complex, Late Archaic/ Early Woodland period, 1500–1000 B.C. (cat. no. 12).

Plate 19. Popeyed Birdstone, banded slate, Red Ocher/Glacial Kame complex, Late Archaic/Early Woodland period, 1500–500 B.C. (cat. no. 13).

Plate 20. Gorget, cannel coal, Glacial Kame complex, Late Archaic/Early Woodland period, 1500–500 B.C. (cat. no. 14).

Plate 21. Sandal-Sole Gorget, marine shell, Glacial Kame complex, Late Archaic/Early Woodland period, 1500–500 B.C. (cat. no. 15).

blades. Certain blade types, such as Wadlow and Etley points, are characteristic of this complex. The fact that these blade types have appeared occasionally at multi-component habitation sites such as Modoc Rock Shelter and Koster in Illinois suggests that the complex may be dated about 2000 B.C. (Roper 1978). Since the vast majority of Titterington sites are mortuary, however, the proposal that a Titterington "phase" be inserted into the Late Archaic chronology may be premature.

Red Ocher and Glacial Kame are two Great Lakes burial complexes that seem to reflect slightly varying patterns of access to exotic trade goods, or goods from distant areas. Both complex names refer strictly to mortuary components. Red Ocher is defined by three distinctive traits: large ceremonial knives made of fine white chipped chert, ovate or triangular blades found in caches, and a distinctive projectile point type made of Harrison County hornstone and known as a "turkey-tail" blade because of its unusual base (Ritzenthaler and Quimby 1962:249) **(fig. 3)**. Glacial Kame, on the other hand, is defined primarily by the appearance of a distinctive marine-shell ornament known as a sandal-sole gorget **(pl. 21)** because its shape suggests that of a sandal

Opposite:
Figure 3. Turkey-tail point, Harrison County hornstone. Late Archaic period, 1500–500 B.C.

Plate 22. Two Rectangular Gorgets, quartz, Early Woodland period, 1000–500 B.C. (cat. no. 16.1–.2).

Plate 23. Locust-Shaped Bead, red jasper, Poverty Point culture, Late Archaic period, 1500–700 B.C. (cat. no. 17).

sole (Cunningham 1948). Both complexes share many attributes: burials covered with red ocher, copper beads and awls, marine-shell beads, tubular pipes, birdstones (an *atlatl* weight shaped like a bird) **(pls. 16–19)**, and ground slate ornaments. While there is some overlap in geographic range, Glacial Kame sites tend to be distributed in Lower Michigan, Ohio, and Ontario, while Red Ocher sites are most abundant in Indiana, Illinois, and Wisconsin. This pattern no doubt reflects differential access to trade routes for specific materials, with marine shell being directed to the interior from the east and southern coasts for Glacial Kame, and Red Ocher having proximity to sources of chert in Indiana, Illinois, and Missouri. The cultural systems that supported these two complexes were clearly related, if not identical.

Little is known about the settlement patterns associated with the Red Ocher/Glacial Kame complexes. Some later Red Ocher sites in Illinois include so-called Marion-tradition pottery, an Early Woodland ware, while different artifact types relate the Red Ocher/Glacial Kame complexes to the New York State Meadowood and early Point Peninsula phases and the beginnings of the Adena cultural pattern in Ohio, Kentucky, and West Virginia, all traditionally regarded as Early Woodland. In fact, the more the question is analyzed, the more any clear demarcation

Plate 24. Three Owl-Effigy Beads, jasper, Poverty Point culture, Late Archaic period, 1500–700 B.C. (left and right: cat. no. 18.1–.2; center: private collection).

between the end of the Late Archaic and the beginning of the Early Woodland period seems artificial.

The same situation exists in the South, where the phrase "Pickwick Burial complex" is used to describe mortuary sites containing many types of trade materials: shell beads and pendants, steatite bowls, stone ornaments and bannerstones **(pl. 11)**, and tools and blades of various kinds (Walthall 1980:91–95). Some northern material appears among Pickwick burials, including Indiana hornstone, copper beads, and galena, but this is rare. The Pickwick complex encompasses the end of the Lauderdale phase; Poverty Point; the fiber-tempered-pottery-producing Stallings Island and Orange cultures; the succeeding Wheeler phase (1300–500 B.C.), which also produced fiber-tempered pottery; and perhaps even the early Alexander tradition (500–100 B.C.) **(fig. 4)**, thus extending well into the Early Woodland period.

The Late Archaic period began, then, with the gradual emergence of new economic strategies and the development of related political and social institutions around 4000–3000 B.C. The economic and social possibilities of the basic cultural patterns established during the Late Archaic continued to grow, uninterrupted, until the Middle Woodland "climax" of 200 B.C.–A.D. 400, without significant changes in settlement patterns and economic strategies.

Plate 25. Animal-Effigy Bead, jasper, Poverty Point culture, Late Archaic period, 1500–700 B.C. (cat. no. 19).

Opposite:
Plate 28. Engraved Plummet Showing a Bird, red jasper, Poverty Point culture, Late Archaic period, 1500–700 B.C. (cat. no. 22).

Plate 26. Clamshell-Effigy Bead, jasper, Poverty Point culture, Late Archaic period, 1500–700 B.C. (cat. no. 20).

Plate 27. Blade-Shaped Pendant, red jasper, Poverty Point culture, Late Archaic period, 1500–700 B.C. (cat. no. 21).

Plate 30. Human Figurine, terra cotta, Poverty Point culture, Late Archaic period, 1500–700 B.C. (cat. no. 24).

Plate 29. Plummet, hematite, Poverty Point culture, Late Archaic period, 1500–700 B.C. (cat. no. 23).

II. THE WOODLAND PERIOD

David S. Brose

As we have seen, the Late Archaic period was characterized by the establishment of a variety of regional settlement and subsistence systems in a range of environments. For two generations American archaeologists have compared the cultural stage of the Archaic with that of the European Mesolithic. The Woodland period has been seen as related to the Neolithic economic "revolution" because of the presence of agriculture, ceramics, and village life.

It should be clear, however, that there may be problems with definitions of the Woodland period that are based on the presence of agriculture and ceramics or on the assumption of at least seasonal sedentism. Some have equated the Woodland era with the practice of burial mound construction. Many of these conditions could be found in one or another Late Archaic society to some degree, however. Furthermore, agriculture did not become significant until after A.D. 700. Ceramics, traditionally recognized as diagnostic artifacts differentiating the Late Archaic from the Early Woodland, in fact had little economic impact when they appeared at Early Woodland sites. Both the Late Archaic and Early Woodland periods were characterized by long-distance trade of exotic artifacts and materials and by special mortuary practices that differentiated between the status of individuals. As has been mentioned in the previous chapter, trade systems may have functioned to maintain access to distant territories in case of shortfalls in regionally available resources, which seem to have occurred cyclically. Although the quality and quantity of trade material circulated through these systems of exchange altered over time, similar patterns of economic activity and resulting socio-economic conditions characterized both Late Archaic and Woodland social groups until about A.D. 700.

Clear distinctions are also lacking between Late Archaic and Early Woodland burial complexes. Inclusion of the Red Ocher, Glacial Kame, and Old Copper complexes of the Great Lakes region in the Archaic period and of the Adena, Hopewell, and Marion complexes, as well as—by implication—the Deptford, Swift Creek, Santa Rosa, and Marksville cultures of the Southeast in the following Woodland period implies significant changes or differences between the two groups. This, as we shall see, is misleading.

Plate 31. *Wilmington Tablet*, sandstone, Late Adena culture, Middle Woodland period, 400 B.C.–A.D. 1 (cat. no. 25).

Plate 32. *Berlin Tablet*, sandstone, Late Adena culture, Middle Woodland period, 400 B.C.–A.D. 1 (cat. no. 26).

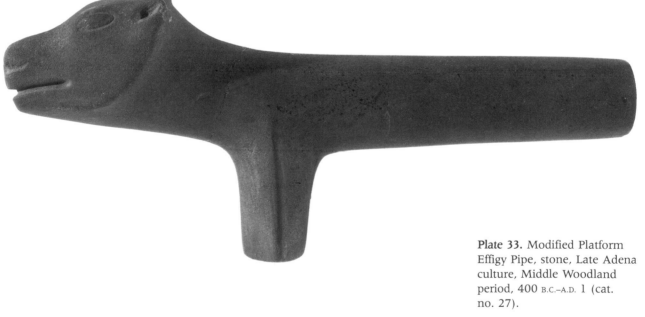

Plate 33. Modified Platform Effigy Pipe, stone, Late Adena culture, Middle Woodland period, 400 B.C.–A.D. 1 (cat. no. 27).

Plate 34. Hand-Shaped Cutout, sheet mica, Ohio Hopewell culture, Middle Woodland period, 200 B.C.–A.D. 400 (cat. no. 28).

44

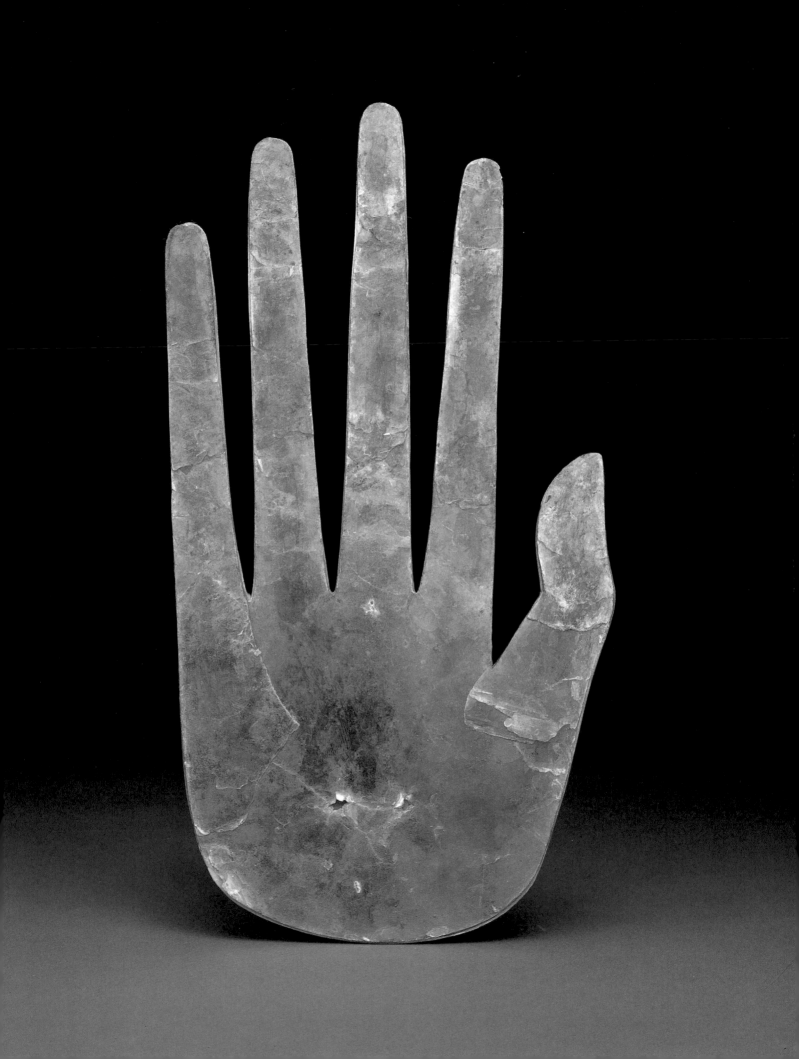

Plate 35. Bird-Claw-Shaped Cutout, sheet mica, Ohio Hopewell culture, Middle Woodland period, 200 B.C.– A.D. 400 (cat. no. 29).

The period between 500 B.C. and A.D. 500 was, in fact, one of transition and development. Regionally distinct patterns of economic subsistence and styles of material culture appeared throughout the Midwest and Southeast. Patterns of mortuary ritual emerged that created the foundations of funerary ceremonialism throughout the area for the next two thousand years. Yet Early Woodland ceremonial activities did not only involve a continuation of Late Archaic traditions. New artifact styles and raw materials and innovations in mortuary ritual reveal significant shifts in exchange networks and concomitant inter-regional cultural relationships.

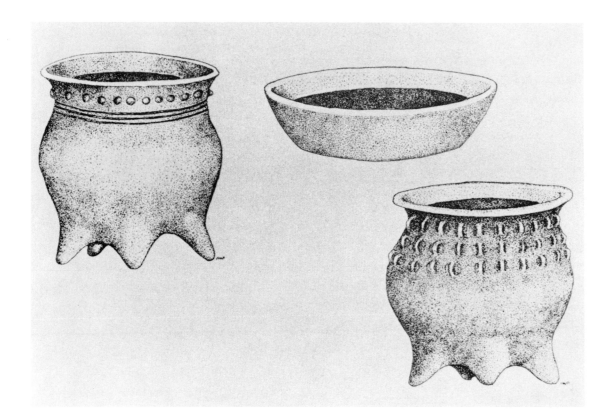

Figure 4. Vessels, ceramic. Alexander complex. Early Woodland period, 500–100 B.C. Reproduced from Walthall 1980:101.

The Early Woodland Complexes

Sometime shortly after 500 B.C., stylistic influences clearly derived from several differing ceramic and ceremonial traditions appear to have coalesced into four regionally differing cultural complexes: Alexander, in the middle Tennessee River valley; Tchefuncte, in the lower Mississippi River valley; Morton, in the central and lower Illinois River valley; and Adena, in the middle and upper Ohio River valley (pls. 31–33). It was the interaction of these regional archaeological traditions that served to highlight the development after 200 B.C. of the Early Woodland period into what will be called here the Middle Woodland.

Alexander pottery combines the northeastern concept of separating the base, body, and rim of a vessel into different decorative fields with the Gulf Coast preference for zoned decorative compositions textured with dentate rocker stamping or punctations. Complex rectilinear patterns ornament thin, well-fired, globular jars with everted rims (fig. 4). Continuities of ceramic style existed between the Alexander heartland of the Tennessee valley and the Mobile Bay and Delta region of the Gulf. Alexander pottery thereby influenced the ceramic development of the Gulf Coast, having been introduced to the Bayou la Batré and Tchefuncte complexes

47

of Mobile Bay and the lower Mississippi valley by 500 B.C. The Alexander, Bayou la Batré, and Tchefuncte sites all reveal a pattern of seasonal reoccupation (i.e., the regularly repeated use of given sites) involving broad-based hunting and gathering activities as well as a significant continual harvesting of shellfish (Walthall 1980:95–103).

In all of these Gulf complexes, most burials consisted either of flexed individuals in simple pits or of masses of reburied bone bundles. At a few larger, reoccupied sites, multiple burials were covered with low earthen mounds. Tchefuncte interments included Arkansas quartz crystals; plummets of stone or hematite; Florida conch shells worked into gouges; copper beads; cut and perforated animal jaws and canine teeth; alligator teeth; and Alabama chert and quartzite. More rare were tubular, fired-clay pipes, occasionally with flared ends and—still more rarely—with incised designs. Equally unusual were Tchefuncte ceramics, which had sand and fired-clay temper added to the clay paste for strength. Despite the fact that they were poorly fired and often carelessly executed, these ceramics display a variety of shapes and design motifs, which were executed by incising, pinching, or punctating; by rocker, dentate, or—rarely—paddle stamping; and by occasional painting in red. The mortuary ceremonialism and expanding network of trade sources along the Gulf during this period anticipated the cultural patterns of the Middle Woodland (Ford and Quimby 1945).

The Early Woodland populations of the central Illinois Morton complex inhabited seasonally reoccupied sites on the terrace edges of the Illinois River and its major tributaries. Seasonally restricted hunting and gathering camps also were established out on the flood plain or up in the interfluvial highlands. Although no domestic or other structures are known for the Morton groups, the contemporary Baumer complexes of southern Illinois had roughly squared houses made with rows of wooden posts. Morton burial ritual differed from the earlier Red Ocher by the apparent standardization of flexed or extended group burials in pits or log crypt tombs beneath earth mounds. Some individuals were sprinkled liberally with red ocher and equipped with copper pins, points, beads, breastplates, tubes, finely chipped turkey-tail blades (fig. 3), sandal-sole gorgets of marine shell (pl. 21), and ground fragments of hematite or galena (Cole and Deuel 1937). Groups of these kinds of objects were also placed in mounds as isolated caches. Morton ceramics blend northeastern manufacturing techniques and vessel shapes with stamped, punctated, and zoned, incised geometric designs derived from the lower Mississippi valley and central Gulf Coast. This Illinois/lower Mississippi axis of cultural contact expanded during the Middle Woodland period,

Plate 36. Human Profile Cutout, sheet mica, Ohio Hopewell culture, Middle Woodland period, A.D. 200–400 (cat. no. 30).

48

when the Illinois Havana and Louisiana Marksville traditions shared significant aspects of pottery design and decoration.

The Adena complex (**pls. 31–33**), within the middle and upper Ohio valley, was certainly the most visibly elaborate of the Early Woodland societies. Carbon 14 dates of objects found at Adena sites range from 1100 B.C. to A.D. 700. Attempts to develop chronological phases within Adena have been based on changes in ceramic styles, the types of bases fashioned for projectile points, and even the complexity of mound construction. No one of these chronologies has met with universal acceptance, however; even within small portions of the region they have resulted in conflicting site sequences.

Plate 37. Eagle-Shaped Cutout, copper, Ohio Hopewell culture, Middle Woodland period, 200 B.C.–A.D. 400 (cat. no. 31).

Adena sites can be divided into three major centers from west to east within the Ohio valley: one area at the mouths of the Kentucky, Great and Little Miami, and Licking rivers; another area around the mouths of the Scioto, Big Sandy, and Muskingum rivers; and a third around the mouths of the Kanawha, Hocking, and Beaver rivers. These divisions became especially significant between at least 250 B.C. and A.D. 250.

Adena earthworks and mounds appear as simple circular embankments and conical burial mounds, some—such as the sixty-seven-foot-high mound in Miamisburg, Ohio, or the seventy-

Plate 38. Falcon-Shaped Cut-out, copper, Ohio Hopewell culture, Middle Woodland period, 200 B.C.–A.D. 1 (cat. no. 32).

one-foot-high Grave Creek mound in West Virginia—achieving an impressive size. Adena mounds, like many smaller Early Woodland ones, reveal several stages of sub-mound construction built on top of a single, circular structure, which had been burned over a central, rectangular, often log-lined pit containing burials (Webb and Snow 1945; Otto 1971, 1979).

Adena sub-mound mortuary structures exceed a hundred feet in diameter. Nearly all of these appear to have been circular houses, possibly with out-slanted walls. If these were ceremonial structures, there is little evidence for what domestic structures might have been. A nearly square house without burials dating from sometime after the Early Woodland period was found associated with small Adena mounds at a site just north of Columbus, Ohio (Webb and Snow 1945; Otto 1979).

Information assembled from mounds, dry caves, and—rarely—from village or camp sites suggests a broad and diffuse pattern of hunting, fishing, and gathering at this time. Squash, pumpkin, sunflowers, goosefoot, and marsh elder were all being grown for seeds. Adena pottery from the Ohio valley consists of bulbous, cylindrical jars with plain or cord-marked surfaces and little decoration, save for some diagonal slashing and rare check-stamping or

51

Plate 39. Cutout Plaque, copper, Ohio Hopewell culture, Middle Woodland period, 200 B.C.–A.D. 1 (cat. no. 33).

Plate 40. Repoussé Plaque Showing Four Birds, copper, Ohio Hopewell culture, Middle Woodland period, 200 B.C.–A.D. 1 (cat. no. 34).

patterning in incised, nested rhomboids. The latter is similar to the Lake Borgne Incised style of Tchefuncte pottery.

Although the spread of ceramics and the development of regional ceramic types are two of the cultural characteristics of the Early Woodland period, it seems that pottery did not accompany the dead into the hereafter, although it was used in graveside rituals. Cut animal teeth and jaws (some used as maskettes); gorgets of polished stone or copper in a range of shapes, including rectangular (pl. 22) and reel-shaped examples; stone and fired-clay pipes in several tubular styles; and caches of points and blades of exotic stone were all common as grave goods, however. Copper rings and bracelets, cloth-wrapped copper celts or points, mica crescents, and alligator teeth occurred rarely. Other objects more common to a variety of Early Woodland contexts included ground or abraded hemispheres, plummets, small rectangular celts of hematite, and ground lumps or crystals of galena.

The stone pallet is considered to have been characteristic of the Ohio valley Adena societies. Stone tablets existed throughout the eastern Woodlands during this period. Most are simple rectangles, although a few have zoomorphic-effigy appendages. A small group from the Ohio valley is engraved with designs composed of broad lines that may be interpreted as highly stylized raptorial birds (pls. 31, 32). Without question the traces of pigment on these tablets suggest their use as stamps, possibly for decorating perishable organic materials such as cloth, articles of clothing, or bark house walls. Similar carved representations appear on a bowl cut from a human skull unearthed at the Adena mound in Florence, Ohio. In rare instances, comparable designs have been found on southern ceramics such as a zoned, punctated bowl from the Tchefuncte site at Big Oak Island or a Late Deptford/Early Swift Creek jar with a complicated stamp design from Fairchild's Landing, Georgia. While the iconography of the Adena engraved tablets was widely distributed toward the end of the Early Woodland period, the tablets themselves were not. They are all from sites concentrated along the middle and upper Ohio River or the lower courses of its major tributaries.

Tubular tobacco pipes appeared during the Late Archaic period as polished stone tubes or simple, tapered cylinders. Adena pipes offer an apparent stylistic progression from blocked-end tubular forms to ones with flaring ends. The latter, such as the shoveler-duck-head pipes from the Welcome mound in West Virginia, occasionally exhibit zoomorphic carvings at the wider end. The fully sculpted figural pipe from the Adena mound (fig. 5) represents the culmination of this trend. The modified platform pipe, a tubular type with a perpendicular stem extension in the middle, is a rare Adena form, very likely influenced by the later Ohio Hope-

Plate 41. Eagle-Effigy Boatstone, pipestone and river
pearl, Ohio Hopewell culture,
Middle Woodland period,
200 B.C.–A.D. 400 (cat. no. 35).

Plate 42. Duck-Effigy Boat-
stone, stone, Ohio Hopewell,
Middle Woodland period,
A.D. 1–400 (cat. no. 36).

Opposite:
Figure 5. Human-effigy pipe,
pipestone, h. 20 cm. Adena
mound, Ross County, Ohio.
Early Woodland period, 500
B.C.–A.D. 1. Photo: Ohio Historical Society, Columbus.

Plate 43. Horned-Monster-Effigy Boatstone, stone, Ohio Hopewell Culture, Middle Woodland period, A.D. 200–400 (cat. no. 37).

Plate 44. Bird-Head-Effigy Carving, garnet-mica schist, Ohio Hopewell culture, Middle Woodland period, A.D. 100–300 (cat. no. 38).

well platform pipes **(pls. 46,47)**. In at least one instance a modified platform pipe included a sculpted bear head at the distal end **(pl. 33)**.

In many ways the close of the Early Woodland represented a major change from the more egalitarian societies of the Late Archaic. An increase in ceremonial trade and activities resulted in fewer major exchange systems. New quotidian objects and ritual iconography were added to the repertoire of several Early Woodland societies. There were greater distinctions of status within those societies involved in ritual exchange, since some individuals may have acquired enhanced status through these expanded social and economic processes.

The Middle Woodland Period

Unfortunately, though understandably, for many regions of eastern North America, archaeologists have relied upon changes in ceramics to identify the onset of the Middle Woodland period. Beginning about 150 B.C. within the southern Tchefuncte and Bayou la Batré societies, there was a shift in ceramic decor and technique that resulted in several new pottery types. These are characterized by zones filled with rocker or dentate stamping set off from plain fields by broad, incised, curvilinear lines. This technique created the appearance of negative and positive surfaces (Jenkins 1981). After 100 B.C. these new designs are called Marksville in the lower

Mississippi valley, Porter in the Mobile Bay region, and Havana in central Illinois (fig. 6; pls. 56–58, 67). All are considered to have been typical of the Middle Woodland period. These and other regional cultures of this era are frequently equated with the large earthwork sites and ceremonial activities of the Ohio Hopewell tradition that were centered around the Chillicothe region of southern Ohio (fig. 31). Although some relationships between these regional complexes and the Ohio Hopewell did exist, each is better characterized by its own unique regional aspects.

The Ohio Hopewell may have been the most complex of all of the "Hopewellian" Middle Woodland regional traditions of eastern North America. It may also be the least understood; certainly it is the least accurately dated. Ohio Hopewell sites in the Scioto River valley date from as early as 100 B.C. to as late as A.D. 600. Their variability is expressed in virtually every aspect of archaeologically recovered data (Caldwell and Hall 1964; Brose and Greber 1979).

The monumental systems of mounds and embankments clustered along the Scioto River are among the most impressive

Figure 6. Vessel showing bird design, ceramic, h. 11 cm, diam. 8.2 cm. Marksville site, Avoyelles Parish, Louisiana. Middle Woodland period, A.D. 1–200. Photo: The National Museum of Natural History, Smithsonian Institution, Washington, D.C.

Plate 45. Kneeling Male Figurine, terra cotta, Ohio Hopewell culture, Middle Woodland period, A.D. 200–400 (cat. no. 39).

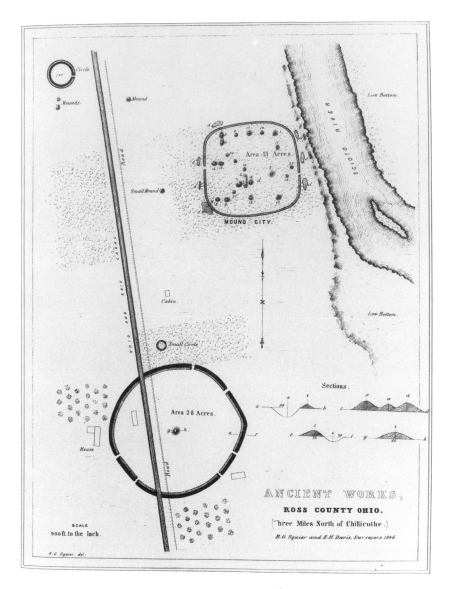

Figure 7. Plan of the Mound City site and vicinity prepared by G. E. Squier and E. H. Davis. Reproduced from Squier and Davis 1848: pl. 19.

Figure 8. View of the Mound City site, Chillicothe, Ohio.

Plate 46. Coyote-Effigy Platform Pipe, pipestone, Ohio Hopewell culture, Middle Woodland period, 200 B.C.–A.D. 100 (cat. no. 40).

Plate 47. Falcon-Effigy Platform Pipe, pipestone and river pearl, Ohio Hopewell culture, Middle Woodland period, 200 B.C.–A.D. 100 (cat. no. 41).

Plate 48. Beaver-Effigy Platform Pipe, pipestone, river pearl, and bone, Havana culture, Middle Woodland period, 100 B.C.–A.D. 200 (cat. no. 42).

Plate 49. Bear-Effigy Platform Pipe, pipestone and copper, Crab Orchard culture, Middle Woodland period, 200 B.C.–A.D. 200 (cat. no. 43).

Plate 50. Cardinal-Effigy Platform Pipe, red sandstone, Crab Orchard culture, Middle Woodland period, 200 B.C.–A.D. 200 (cat. no. 44).

and perplexing Ohio Hopewell phenomena. Geometric earthworks occur as squares, circles, octagons, ellipses, and trapezoids, and as straight or curved parallel lines. They may be isolated, arranged in sets of one or two of each shape, or arrayed in complexes including all of these shapes. There are also isolated examples of irregular shapes or of stylized zoomorphic ones. The earthworks, which cover areas ranging from two to 1,320 acres in size, may be mathematically precise or rather careless in appearance (Thomas 1894; Shetrone 1930). Many display an extraordinary correspondence of alignments (fig. 7), suggesting seasonal solar and/or lunar orientations (Brose 1976; Greber 1983).

A great number of the larger earthworks contain anywhere from one to twenty-two burial mounds (Squier and Davis 1848), while some earthworks contain none. Mounds within or outside of earthworks may be placed in geometrically precise locations or may be uniformly or randomly located. The burial mounds themselves can be loaf-shaped, conical, or even like truncated pyramids, and range from under one thousand to nearly one million cubic feet in volume (fig. 8). The burials contained in some of them may be wholly or partially cremated, in place or not, and may consist of extended or flexed in-flesh burials (i.e., burials of intact bodies) or piles of partially or wholly disarticulated bones or even isolated skulls or parts of skulls. Burials of individuals or groups (Greber 1976) may occur in pits below or dug through any of several floor layers; the pits may be unlined or lined with clay, skins, logs, slabs of bark, limestone, or mica. Burials are also found laid directly on the floor or on small raised platforms of stone, logs and bark, or clay. Burials may be covered with small mounds of earth, sterile sand, clay, or gravel, or with slabs of limestone or mica—or left uncovered. In fact, some burials were placed on or into these small mounds. In several of them, different floors of variously colored earth separate sequences of mortuary activity (Greber 1983).

All of these activities may have taken place within structures or rooms, which were circular, square, or trapezoidal in shape. Some of these structures or rooms seem to have decayed in place; some seem to have been pulled down, while others were burned (J. A. Brown 1979). Rooms, structures, and/or primary mounds were sometimes enclosed within overlapping or separated secondary mounds, and some sets of secondary mounds were further enclosed in larger final mounds, which had caps of red or white sand or clay, river gravels, or large stone slabs (Shetrone 1930).

Given the incredible variety of mound and mortuary treatment, very few valid generalizations about Ohio Hopewell funer-

Plate 51. Raven-Effigy Platform Pipe, conglomerate, Crab Orchard culture, Middle Woodland period, 200 B.C.–A.D. 200 (cat. no. 45).

ary ceremonialism can be made. In fact, it is only the nature and use of deliberately included offerings that tie Ohio Hopewell sites together. Among the most important of such offerings were objects made of copper: celts and axes ranging from two inches to more than three feet in length; bicymbal, or yo-yo-shaped, ear spools; large breastplates, gorgets, and headdresses; and—in a few important burials—plaques or cutout silhouettes in a variety of curvilinear shapes or in the form of birds, reptiles, or mammals **(figs. 25, 32; pls. 37–40)**. Sheet mica, which was rare at Adena sites, appears in Ohio Hopewell contexts as roughly cut sheets or occasional cutouts and silhouettes representing serpents; raptors' talons; human torsos; profiled human faces; and human hands **(fig. 28; pls. 34–36)**. Small stone platform pipes having thin, curved platforms for stems and cylindrical or carved effigy bowls in their centers were also typical **(pls. 46, 47)**. The great majority of them came from either the Tremper or Mound City sites, where they were grouped in burned caches numbering well over a hundred pipes. Sculpted boatstones, small carvings with their interiors hollowed out on one side, display a similar iconography of birds and animals executed in a remarkably naturalistic style (pls. 41–43). Cut animal and human jaws, obsidian blades (fig. 27), bear canines, river pearls, and marine-shell beads and cups also are found frequently with burials.

These items and the ritual roles which can be posited for them serve to identify the cultural ties between the Ohio Hopewell and a series of distinct social groups spread across the continent. This system of cultural contacts has been called the Hopewell Interaction Sphere, although the term conveys little beyond the fact that a series of distinct types of raw materials and artifacts was somehow widely dispersed throughout the eastern Woodlands (Caldwell and Hall 1964; Brose and Greber 1979).

As in earlier periods, the major vectors of exchange were composed of Great Lakes copper moving south and Gulf Coast marine shell moving north, although this trade was intensified during the Middle Woodland. The increasing importance of mica obtained from the Southeast appears to have been balanced by the establishment of new sources of materials in the Northwest, such as Yellowstone River obsidian, Rocky Mountain grizzly bear teeth, and Knife River chalcedony (a translucent variety of quartz) from the Dakotas. The exchange of hematite, galena, and quartz crystals from sources in the South and East continued and may have increased during the Middle Woodland period. So did the movement north and west of such natural curiosities as shark, alligator, and gar (a freshwater fish) teeth collected from the southern Atlantic and Gulf coasts. Multicolored Ohio Flint Ridge chalcedony entered this exchange system in the form of thin, narrow prismatic blades struck from carefully prepared cores. A somewhat cruder Illinois blade technology existed, although its products (however they were used) do not appear to have been as widely distributed as those from Ohio. However, the Illinois Snyder's point, a deeply corner-notched, convex-sided equilateral triangle, occurred both in caches and, west of Ohio, in the form of local reproductions.

To some extent the ceremonial role taken by the naturalistically sculpted or modeled stone and clay pipes (pls. 46, 47) and statuettes (pl. 45) from Ohio must have been prescribed by the forms and structures of the rituals of inter-group exchange and group burial that already had been accepted by other social groups. As we shall see, the ultimate use of these objects constitutes one of the few nearly consistent patterns across the Middle Woodland, suggesting that they were widely perceived as carrying a powerful and commonly accepted ideological message concerning relationships between society and the natural and supernatural worlds. While there appear to have been several distinct geographic patterns of Hopewellian exchange, one of the

Plate 52. Seated Human Figurine, terra cotta, Havana culture, Middle Woodland period, 50 B.C.–A.D. 250 (cat. no. 46).

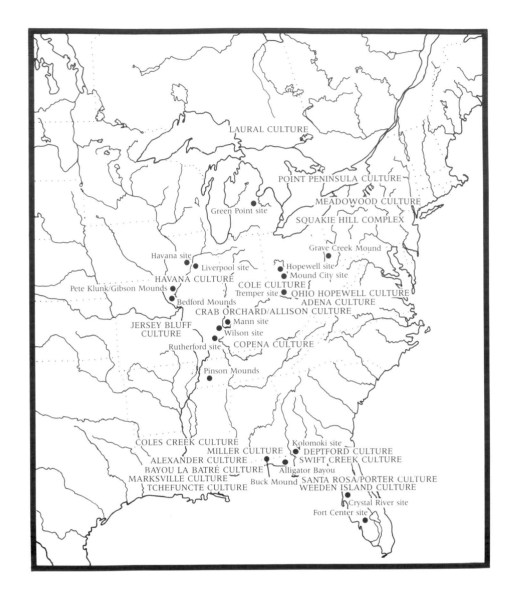

LAURAL CULTURE

POINT PENINSULA CULTURE

MEADOWOOD CULTURE

Green Point site

SQUAKIE HILL COMPLEX

Grave Creek Mound

Havana site

Liverpool site

HAVANA CULTURE

Hopewell site

Mound City site

COLE CULTURE

Pete Klunk/Gibson Mounds

Tremper site

OHIO HOPEWELL CULTURE

Bedford Mounds

ADENA CULTURE

CRAB ORCHARD/ALLISON CULTURE

JERSEY BLUFF
CULTURE

Mann site

Wilson site

Rutherford site

COPENA CULTURE

Pinson Mounds

COLES CREEK CULTURE

Kolomoki site

MILLER CULTURE

DEPTFORD CULTURE

ALEXANDER CULTURE

SWIFT CREEK CULTURE

BAYOU LA BATRE CULTURE

Alligator Bayou

MARKSVILLE CULTURE

Buck Mound

SANTA ROSA/PORTER CULTURE

TCHEFUNCTE CULTURE

WEEDEN ISLAND CULTURE

Crystal River site

Fort Center site

Woodland period sites and
culture areas.

more distinctive aspects of this distribution pattern was its lack of
spatial continuity. Areas of intense Hopewellian exchange activity
were surrounded by far larger areas of non-Hopewellian Middle
Woodland sites (Brose and Greber 1979). The reasons for this remain unknown.

Outside the Hopewellian core of south-central Ohio, a second major region of related Middle Woodland activity existed
several hundred miles to the west. It comprised the Havana complexes, spread across central and western Illinois, and the Crab
Orchard/Allison complexes, located in the southern and eastern
portions of that state and extending into the southeastern tributaries of the Wabash River. These complexes have been differentiated primarily on the basis of the surface finish on most domestic

ceramics and by slight typological variations in ceremonial pieces. This Illinois pottery (pls. 56–58), unlike the Hopewellian-style pottery in Ohio (fig. 31), clearly shows a formal and technological development from the local late Early Woodland Morton or early Crab Orchard ceramics. Indeed, at a time when archaeological interpretations saw "Hopewell" as a single ethnic group or culture, it was the gradual nature of ceramic change in Illinois which suggested that "Hopewell" in fact had originated there during the first few centuries B.C. To the extent that reliable radiocarbon dates are available, there is no clear chronological priority for either Illinois or Ohio in terms of the mound-centered mortuary rituals involving the exchange of exotic artifacts. However, unlike Ohio Hopewell, there are only one or two large earthworks in Illinois that have been reported as possibly being related to Havana sites, and none are known to be related to Crab Orchard/Allison sites, with the possible exception of Mann, as we shall see.

There are some significant differences between the burial mounds of Ohio and those of Illinois. Within the Havana tradition, the earliest clear Middle Woodland manifestations appear along river bluffs at a few rather large and relatively complex mounds such as those in the Dickinson, Liverpool, Sister Creeks, Ogden-Fettie, or Havana (type-site of the tradition) groups (pl. 56). There often seem to be some associated village remains. The mounds appear to have been constructed in stages. On the stripped ground level, large single- or double-post oval structures contained sand or clay platforms with numerous fired areas and central sub-floor pits and/or log crypt tombs. The tombs contained less than a dozen, usually extended individuals accompanied by few artifacts, most of which appear to have been personal possessions, although ceramic vessels with avian and geometric iconography clearly were included as grave goods (pls. 57, 58).

The middle phases of the Havana tradition are represented by a large number of relatively small and less complex mounds, which occur both on bluffs and terraces in rather large groups (over thirty at some sites), frequently with several associated domestic middens, which have been called villages. The Clear Lake, Knight, Weaver, Hummell, Brangenburg, and some of the Naples, Gibson, and Bedford (pl. 48) mounds have been assigned to this phase with its "classic Hopewellian"-style ceramics. Most of these mounds contain only a single central sub-floor pit, often lined with logs or slabs of bark or stone. Burials generally consist of a few bundled or extended bodies, most again with few grave goods, including whole pottery vessels.

Within the past decade, studies of the Havana sites have suggested that few burials there reflect strong status distinctions and, indeed, that the individual accumulations of grave goods typical in Ohio were characteristically absent in Illinois. Indeed it has been suggested that most, if not all, Havana-tradition individuals received mound burial. The area in which the Crab Orchard/Allison tradition existed shows indications of strong, if temporally limited, Havana influence. The chronological relationships of these two archaeological traditions are imperfectly known within the Wabash valley itself and are still less certain beyond the valley. Their ties, if any, to the Mann site further east are also unclear (Winters 1967:47–52).

At the Wilson mound group along the Wabash River bluffs, nearly all of the log-tomb burials had a few grave goods, such as fabric-wrapped or plain copper celts or awls, cut animal jaws, conch-shell dippers, or animal effigy pipes (pls. 49, 50). Occasional caches of heaped antler tines, hammer stones, and even a copper punch and an antler handle were also found. So too were several complete vessels and numerous fragments of Havana stamped pottery, most of which have been dated to early in the Illinois Hopewell sequence. These mounds were apparently associated with several burials of adults and younger people in a bluff-edge cemetery. The limited grave goods are consistent with a Middle Woodland affiliation. What may be the chronological equivalent of the middle Havana tradition in this area is represented by unclear Havana influence at sites such as that at the rather late Rutherford mound (pl. 51), which has no central pit, but which has numerous disarticulated or cremated individuals on the original, prepared sand ground surface or on the prepared primary mound surface. Equally unusual was the concentration with many burials of exotic grave goods.

The end of the Middle Woodland period presently is defined for southeastern Illinois as around A.D. 450 on the basis of ceramic criteria. At this time there was something of a shift to rather egalitarian (possibly family) burials in stone mounds along the river bluffs. Indeed, throughout western and also in central Illinois, some of the most egalitarian (and largest) of the mounds seem to span the Middle-Late Woodland transition. Across all of the Illinoian Middle Woodland phases and traditions, the grave goods which accompanied burials were similar in kind to those at the Ohio Hopewell sites, although smaller amounts were more equally distributed among the population. Simple animal and human effigy platform pipes of Ohio pipestone (a claylike stone), often with pearl eye insets (pl. 48), are quite commonly found, usually one or two of them with one or two burials in any given mound. Copper ear spools, celts (fig. 24), beads, so-called "panpipes," breastplates, headdress plaques, rings, and bracelets all occur, but again (save at such exceptional sites as Rutherford) generally rather thinly distributed. Galena fragments are ubiquitous. Rec-

Plate 53. Seated Male Figurine, terra cotta, Crab Orchard/Allison culture, Middle Woodland period, A.D. 100–300 (cat. no. 47).

Left:
Plate 54. Seated Female Figurine, terra cotta, Havana culture, Middle Woodland period, A.D. 100–300 (cat. no. 48).

Above:
Plate 55. Human Figurine Fragment, terra cotta, Havana culture, Middle Woodland period, A.D. 100–300 (cat. no. 49).

tangular and reel-shaped gorgets of various exotic stones occur rarely, as do cut marine-shell dippers or cups.

The most common "Hopewellian" artifacts in the Havana-tradition sites include masses of pearls or disk-shaped, marine-shell beads. Geometric or zoomorphic mica cutouts are rare, but large, thick mica "mirrors" do occur with the very common cut and drilled grizzly bear canines; mandibles, or lower jawbones (some with pearl inlays); carnivore or human mandible gorgets; or maskettes made of cut maxillae, or upper jawbones. Caches of Snyder's points, frequently of local southern Illinois chert, are also common. Both obsidian and Knife River chalcedony points are found occasionally as grave goods, although neither is as frequent as the prismatic Ohio Flint Ridge bladelets. At several of the Havana-like mounds along the Wabash valley, males were buried with antler and stone flint-working tool kits.

While there was much variation throughout the Middle Woodland period in Illinois, whether at Havana or Crab Orchard/ Allison sites, the general mortuary pattern is different in degree from that inferred for Ohio Hopewell (Asch et al. 1979; Braun 1979). Recent studies by biophysical archaeologists have revealed that the overall Havana population densities were not dramatically different from those in either the Late Archaic or the latest, non-Mississippian, protohistoric periods between A.D. 1500 and 1700. Most mound groups had five or six mounds and contained about four hundred burials. In all, this is about the same as the population estimated from the villages and campsites known on bluffs and terraces. Buikstra (1976, 1979) has noted that, at least in the well-known lower Illinois valley, there was at any given period more social differentiation in mortuary patterns between flood plain mound sites and bluff-top mound locations than within any single group of mounds, with more ritual energy (expressed in artifacts, grave complexity, or space) expended for males in the former. Her studies have revealed that social roles in Havana-tradition societies were not stratified, but were ranked primarily by age and sex, and that local Middle Woodland populations were genetically distinct and stable (Asch 1976).

Middle Woodland sites showing a Havana-like village and mound pattern do not seem to have occurred south of the mouth of the Ohio River. However, most details of ceramic decoration typical of the Havana tradition are also characteristic of Marksville ceramics in Arkansas, Louisiana, and Mississippi (fig. 6). Many of the Marksville sites, which occur west into Texas and along the Gulf Coast east to the Tombigbee River in southwest Alabama above the delta of Mobile Bay (Toth 1979), are located on broad river terraces within single or concentric semicircular rings of earthworks like those at Poverty Point (fig. 1), the Late Archaic site in the lower Mississippi valley. Marksville burials generally consist of groups of in-flesh individuals placed on a low clay platform and covered with a shallow, rather flat mound. Subsequently the flat surface of the mound served as a platform upon which other burials were placed (rarely, in rectangular subsurface log crypt tombs), resulting in layered accretions as high as twenty-five feet and containing several hundred burials. Grave goods accompanying sets of individuals included copper ear spools, rolled buttons and beads, and (rarely) panpipes; quartz crystals; hematite and galena fragments; and a series of locally produced and rather crudely executed zoomorphic platform pipes.

Along the lower Ohio River, located near the mouths of the Wabash, Tennessee, and Cumberland rivers, the largely untested Mann site represents a complex of mounds and linear and geometric earthworks that covered nearly 440 acres between the first and fifth centuries A.D. This complex is surrounded by as much as a mile of debris and surface habitation features. Limited excavation of a few smaller mounds suggests sub-floor pits and log crypt tombs with in-flesh and redeposited burials, each having a moderate range of Hopewellian grave goods (pl. 61). But the more limited excavation of what may have been domestic areas has yielded comparatively vast quantities of projectile points made of Indiana hornstone; prismatic cores and bladelets of Ohio Flint Ridge flint, obsidian, and quartz crystal; cut copper and mica sheets and scrap; shark teeth; galena fragments; and nearly one hundred fragmented, fully modeled, fired-clay human figurines (cf. pl. 53). Perhaps the most surprising aspect of the Mann site is its clay- and grit-tempered ceramics, which, although apparently manufactured locally, include not only significant proportions of both classic Hopewellian zoned, incised, dentate- and rocker-stamped ceramics similar to those at Havana sites, but a consistently high frequency of carved paddle-stamped techniques and motifs clearly derived from Georgia and Florida. Often even the local cord-marked ceramics bear a scalloped lip treatment, which at this time was more common in the Southeast (Kellar 1979).

The Havana tradition's center in central Illinois appears to have been surrounded by a number of geographically distant, but culturally close neighbors up the Mississippi River valley as far north as the Trempeleau River in west-central Wisconsin and Howard Lake in Minnesota. Related sites occur in eastern Iowa and Missouri and extend west to the area of Kansas City. Havana artifacts (pls. 48, 52, 54–58) and mortuary and settlement patterns spread up the Illinois valley to the Porter complexes of the Kankakee drainage in northwestern Indiana, are found in the lower

Opposite:
Plate 56. Jar (Havana Zoned), terra cotta, Havana culture, Middle Woodland period, 200–100 B.C. (cat. no. 50).

Left:
Plate 57. Jar (Hopewell Zoned Stamped), terra cotta, Havana culture, Middle Woodland period, A.D. 1–200 (cat. no. 51).

Grand River and Muskegon River valleys of west-central Michigan, and reoccur almost unchanged at Green Point, the largest site in the Saginaw River valley of eastern Michigan (Griffin et al. 1970; Fitting 1975; Mason 1981).

A generally low density of subsistence resources was characteristic of the Canadian biotic zone and its Middle Woodland societies, from Laurel—with its clearly Havana-derived ceramics—in the west to Point Peninsula with its Ohio-like concentrations of individual silver- and copper-covered panpipes. With dramatic seasonal differences in resources, population concentrations were widely separated, of short duration, and relied heavily on fish. Virtually all of the securely identified Middle Woodland copper came from this region. However ubiquitous small, glacially dispersed nuggets and use-worn tools of copper may have been, outcrops of native copper had been quarried extensively since the earliest times. Perhaps the existence of a silver source in the Sudbury/Cobalt area of Ontario as well as the close proximity of copper sources explain the fact that while some "Hopewell" goods

Plate 58. Jar (Hopewell Zoned Incised), terra cotta, Havana culture, Middle Woodland period, A.D. 1–200 (cat. no. 52).

accompanied individuals in the Middle Woodland Laurel and Point Peninsula burial mounds, they often took the form of lumps of silver, silver or copper beads, or silver-covered panpipes (Fitting 1979; Spence et al. 1979).

After A.D. 150, trade of distinctive artifacts and materials from the Hopewell centers of southern Ohio **(pls. 34–47)** was directed primarily toward the South and East. This exchange should not be understood as indicative of shared cosmology or ideology or of the

Plate 59. Platform Pipe, serpentine, Middle Woodland period, 200 B.C.–A.D. 400 (cat. no. 53).

rituals in which such concepts were expressed, since southeastern ceremonial patterns during the Middle Woodland period appear to have been quite distinctive.

Hopewellian materials, some—such as Ohio flint and effigy platform pipes—from Ohio itself, but also copper-covered pan-pipes, copper ear spools, occasional breastplates, and zoned, den-tate-rocker-stamped pottery (fig. 31; pl. 67), occur in sporadic burial mounds in the central Southeast, from the Tennessee valley to the Appalachian Mountains. The locations suggest some association with Hopewellian mica mining (Chapman and Keel 1979). Other Hopewellian mortuary sites can be found further south, from northwest Georgia nearly to the Gulf Coast (Jeffries 1976). Galena, quartz crystals, conch-shell dippers, copper breastplates, ear spools, panpipes, and some effigy platform pipes appear with burials in sub-floor pits beneath large mounds. No geometric earthworks are known, although several mounds in the shapes of animals have been reported.

The Copena complex developed in the central Tennessee River valley in Alabama after A.D. 100 from an earlier population, which lived on harvested river mollusks and local nuts, supplemented with hunting. By the second century A.D., large village and mound sites had appeared on the river terraces, and large caverns were being used for mortuary rituals. Copena burial mounds were generally constructed over several clay- or bark-slab-lined sub-floor pits, each containing a number of extended individuals, occasionally accompanied by grave goods. Cremations in clay-covered pits were common in caverns, again with few grave goods. Among these were conch-shell cups and beads; large masses of galena; sheet mica cutouts; copper beads, bracelets, ear spools, celts (fig. 24), breastplates, cut sheets, and reel-shaped gorgets; and small caches of large ceremonial blades made of local chert and pipes of local steatite. Many of the latter are simple elbow pipes, but some were carved as massive tubular or platform pipes with fully sculpted animal and bird effigies (pls. 60–63). These Copena "great pipes" became a popular trade item after the first century A.D. and were exported to Illinois, Indiana (pl. 61), Ohio, and other locations throughout the Midwest (Walthall 1979, 1980:116–131).

Between the first and sixth centuries A.D., large Middle Woodland populations lived in a series of big and small villages extending along the entire Gulf Coast. They utilized a variety of decorative techniques to produce a rich assortment of pottery styles zoned with abstract, curvilinear designs or modeled with naturalistic bird and animal forms (pls. 67, 69). Burial mounds associated with many villages were often constructed in several stages, sometimes with flattened tops, ramps, or causeways,

Plate 60. Falcon-Effigy Pipe, steatite, Copena culture, Middle Woodland period, A.D. 100–400 (cat. no. 54).

Plate 61. Panther-Effigy Pipe, steatite, Allison/Copena culture, Middle Woodland period, A.D. 1–400 (cat. no. 55).

78

Plate 62. Bird-and-Owl-Effigy Great Pipe, steatite, Copena culture, Middle Woodland period, A.D. 100–600 (cat. no. 56).

and—more rarely—with geometric or stylized effigy earthworks covering a hundred or more acres. Individuals were buried by themselves or in groups, sometimes with ceramic beakers, bowls, or jars, which were buried intact or deliberately "killed" during the burial ritual. A few ceramic types appear only as grave goods, such as lantern-like pedestal jars with appliquéd human, animal, or bird effigies on top. They were pierced with crescents, whorls, circles, and ellipses, which were cut out prior to firing, and may have functioned as incense burners **(pl. 69)**. Although the Gulf Coast sites in Alabama and Florida are known by a variety of names, such as Santa Rosa/Swift Creek, Porter, Yent, and Green Point, the complex might better be called Crystal River/Kolomoki, after the larger, better-known sites in northwest Florida and southwest Georgia (Willey 1945; Sears 1977; Brose 1979a).

Equally large and complex sites exist in peninsular Florida, such as Shields and North Murphy Island on the St. Johns River and Fort Center and Big Tonys near the Everglades. These sites contain mounds in a variety of shapes and sizes that reveal a great range of mortuary treatment. For example, the Fort Center site included a wooden charnel platform constructed over a pond and ornamented with posts and lintels carved into striking animal and

79

bird sculptures (pl. 71). Many of these were preserved in the underwater mud, revealing an impressive wood-carving tradition which hints at the richness of Middle Woodland art produced in perishable materials (Willey 1949a, 1949b; Brose 1979a; Sears 1982).

Overall, the patterns of ceremonial activity and ritual exchange appear to have been quite different in Middle Woodland Florida than in the Midwest. Despite the probable Ohio provenance for several specific types of Hopewellian objects and materials, they do not appear with the same kind of concentration as in the Midwest. The exchange patterns of the Florida Middle Woodland seem to have involved the internal circulation of local styles and artifacts rather than the trade of materials from outside the area. The ubiquity of galena and conch-shell cups, dippers, and gouges suggests their probable personal and mundane use, rather than any ritual, status role. The recovery of numerous fragmented and whole clay figurines from domestic middens argues against their having had much ceremonial significance in Florida, although certain classes of ceramic vessels obviously did. These are patterns quite unlike those apparent in the Midwest.

The ceramic influence of Copena can be seen in the Miller I/II complex of the upper Tombigbee and upper Tallahatchee drainages in Mississippi and Alabama. Large groups of small and regularly reused burial mounds (the latter having increased in size over time) contain sub-floor pits with cremations and—occasionally—burned fragments of mica, conch-shell cups, copper panpipes, ear spools, plain platform pipes, and a few ceremonial caches of Snyder's corner-notched projectile points from Illinois. Large sub-mound (or pre-mound) mortuary structures, increasingly extended burials, and accretional sub-mound clay platforms with numerous fires appear to represent a shift in burial practices through time and also correspond to a shift from Copena to the later Marksville tradition.

The variety, size, complex shapes, and overall interrelationships of the mounds at Pinson near Jackson, Tennessee, make that site an anomaly. Few Crystal River/Kolomoki-like sherds occur there, and at least one large mound was an accretional series of flat-topped platforms. A smaller, recently excavated mound has yielded evidence of a mortuary ritual which, in its physical structure as well as its iconography (represented by cut mica objects, engraved human skull rattles, and copper ear spools), duplicates patterns found in south-central Ohio or perhaps in northern Florida, although the contemporaneity of these widespread examples is uncertain (Mainfort 1983). Except for the Chattahoochee River gap, then, the Appalachian crest seems to have been an effective barrier to the dissemination of Hopewellian items or ideas. Few of these appear anywhere on the south Atlantic coastal plain save those which spread eastward into southeast Georgia and northeast Florida from the Florida Gulf Coast.

The Late Woodland Period

There are few instances in which Middle Woodland participation in the Hopewellian exchange was not followed by a rather drab Late Woodland insularity in the centuries after A.D. 500. Traditional explanations for this "cultural decline" have held up poorly in the light of recent archaeological investigations. Biophysical analyses confirm a continuity of Middle and Late Woodland populations, thus contradicting previous hypotheses of migration and invasion. In fact, Late Woodland site occupations increased in frequency and size everywhere.

Plate 63. Owl-Effigy Tubular Pipe, steatite, Copena culture, Middle Woodland period, A.D. 100–600 (cat. no. 57).

The more elaborate manifestations of Middle Woodland exchange in exotic materials such as obsidian, Knife River chalcedony, and Ohio Flint Ridge flint withered in the Late Woodland period. The flow of mica, shark and alligator teeth, meteoric iron and silver, pearls, and pipes stopped. Galena nodules and quartz crystals still trickled east from Missouri and Arkansas. The by-then-ancient movement of Great Lakes copper south and Gulf Coast marine shell north persisted throughout the Late Woodland period, however.

The local interpretation of widespread cosmological images in a variety of media that was a striking characteristic of the preceding half-millenium did not survive during the Late Woodland. Except, as we shall see, for Weeden Island ceramics, pipes from the Cole culture in Ohio and from the Jersey Bluff culture of the American Bottoms area near St. Louis **(pl. 64)**, and an unusual set of widely dispersed, engraved shell gorgets, little of the Hopewellian iconographic tradition appears anywhere in the late Woodland archaeological record.

On the Gulf Coastal plain and south to the Everglades, the Weeden Island burial mounds succeeded the earlier Crystal River/Kolomoki complex. Whereas previously a single mound had included one or a small number of individuals with numerous high-status, often exotic artifacts and a larger number of individuals with few or no such materials, Weeden Island mounds indicate a pattern of several groups of apparently related individuals supplied with large assemblages of only occasionally exotic, but still iconographically significant, objects. Late Weeden Island mounds reveal a pattern of very large numbers of undifferentiated individuals with isolated caches of broken ceramics, often as a pavement on the eastern side of the mound. Lesser numbers of relatively small mounds in groups reverted to small mounds located in areas with older, larger mounds, followed, finally, during the ninth century A.D., by the reuse of the larger mounds themselves (Willey 1949a; Brose and Percy 1974).

Most Late Woodland societies of the lower Mississippi valley and the Gulf Coast exhibited significant, if gradual, changes in ceramic styles. Late Woodland ceramics of west Florida had elaborate ceremonial decoration during the fifth and sixth centuries A.D. This was continued on the technically improved vessels of the early Weeden Island cultures well into the eighth century along the coast and perhaps into the tenth century in Alabama. Decor includes geometric and stylized floral motifs executed in monochrome, bichrome, and polychrome painting and a combination of incising and punctating **(pl. 68)**. Modeled forms of birds and animals were not unusual, although the Buck mound in Fort

Plate 64. Raven-Effigy Pipe, stone, Jersey Bluff culture, Late Woodland period, A.D. 400–900 (cat. no. 58).

Walton, Florida, contained a unique polychrome human-effigy urn (pl. 70). It had been deliberately broken and scattered over the surface of the secondary mound prior to the addition of the final mantle of earth.

There seem to have been relatively abrupt discontinuities in ceramic decoration in the Ohio Hopewell centers during the Late Woodland. The elaborate vessel shapes and application of Hopewellian iconography were discontinued by A.D. 600, leaving only the cord-marked or plain-surfaced jars that had always been their non-mortuary companions. The same trend existed in the Illinois ceramics of the Havana tradition, although there the change occurred earlier and was accompanied by a gradual loss of both stylistic rigidity and precision of technical execution (Brose 1978; Griffin 1978).

The assumption that the early Late Woodland period (A.D. 400–900) represented a "time of cultural decline" in any area of the eastern United States appears unacceptable, then, regardless of the loss of the Hopewell artistic tradition. There was, in many areas, a decreasing emphasis on elaborate or exotic goods as burial furniture. However, few regions did not show a continuation of the cultural patterns established during the late Middle Woodland. Late Woodland sites are not only larger and more frequent;

84

they yield the first good evidence for permanent or semipermanent villages whose economic adaptations appear to have been designed to maximize agricultural production. Simple mound and cemetery burial both occurred, and while the distinctions among burial locations probably reflected some structuring of social roles, if not of status, these Late Woodland societies yield little evidence for any exchange of raw materials, finished artifacts, or iconography.

Although characterized by cord-marked and plain ceramics, Late Woodland groups in the central Mississippi valley and related complexes from the southern Ozarks to the Caddoan area show few indications of social stratification or long-distance trade. In these cases there is little evidence even for horticulture. Most sites consist of two or three circular houses, which were occupied seasonally, along river back-swamps or bayous where hunting and gathering were the major subsistence activities. Much the same simple social ecology and material culture seems to be represented by the early Late Woodland societies found further up the Mississippi and Missouri rivers and up the Ohio River valley and its tributaries at least onto the western slopes of the Appalachian plateau.

There is a constant, but rather low, level of exotic material, primarily Gulf Coast conch dippers, found with burials throughout Late Woodland societies across the Gulf Lakes into the Northeast and middle Atlantic coast. Some copper was also traded from the Lake Superior sources east as far as the lower Hudson, but it usually appears as used tools in village middens. Burial patterns within this region after A.D. 700 show a gradual change from small to very large group cemeteries, many with evidence of a few altered or mutilated secondary burials.

From the end of the eleventh century A.D., reburial of bundles of re-articulated bones in massive tribal ossuaries characterized highly egalitarian mortuary rituals. These were initiated by village relocations at ten- or fifteen-year intervals. It is worth pointing out that although early European observers reported the existence of socio-political status positions within these societies during the sixteenth century, almost no reflection of them occurs in the burial patterns (Brose 1978; Mason 1981). In this respect, as in their retention and elaboration of the mound-centered mortuary ritual and representations of a cosmological iconography in pottery decoration (pl. 70), the Weeden Island culture is an exception. It may have been the failure to establish any significant agricultural subsistence base on the salt-sprayed, sandy soils along the Gulf that necessitated the continuation of the inter-group exchange systems (with their socio-economic characteristics) that were the hallmark of the Middle Woodland period. A similar development

Plate 66. Three Bird-Effigy Plummets, stone, Deptford culture, Middle Woodland period, 400 B.C.–A.D. 1 (cat. no. 60.1–.3).

Plate 67. Zoned Jar (Alligator Bayou Stamped), ceramic, Porter/Santa Rosa culture, Middle Woodland period, 100 B.C.–A.D. 400 (cat. no. 61).

Plate 68. Castellated Vessel (Weeden Island Incised), ceramic, Weeden Island culture, Late Woodland period, A.D. 400–900 (cat. no. 62).

occurred with the Late Woodland Coles Creek complex of the lower Mississippi valley (Phillips et al. 1951; Phillips 1970).

Without question, however, there was a change from Middle Woodland concepts of burial mounds as family, or possibly lineage, monuments to a Late Woodland concept of mounds as a focus of multilineage social cohesion. This shift reflected a more basic change from a ritual that rewarded or supported those who had achieved status through their personal efforts to one that emphasized the individual who had been designated by the familial/political group to mediate between society and cosmic/spiritual beings. There was also a coincident change from the mobile, diffuse hunting/fishing/gathering economies of the Middle Woodland to the relatively permanent agricultural societies that presaged the Mississippian period.

Late Woodland and Mississippian societies, by their adoption of an economy based on agriculture, opened themselves up to greater ecological vulnerability. This condition could not be miti-

Plate 69. Bird-Effigy Vessel, ceramic, Crystal River/Kolomoki culture, Middle Woodland period, A.D. 1–500 (cat. no. 63).

gated by developing external social networks as long as other societies were equally vulnerable. In situations where relationships with friends and neighbors are of little help, one naturally looks to the powers that regulate the world itself. This explains much of the increase in hereditary social status and ceremonial, cosmological, and geographic inflexibility from the Late Woodland and Mississippian periods up until the protohistoric era. While any individual could build the social connections of the Early Woodland exchange networks and mortuary rituals, those few persons of the Late Woodland and Mississippian societies who were capable of renewing harmony between the social and cosmic worlds had to be born to the task. To some degree Late Woodland restrictive social mobility also seems to have limited access to cosmological iconography and to have resulted in constricted decorative styles and techniques. To what extent those areas which retained socioeconomic flexibility also maintained artistic spontaneity remains to be explored.

Plate 70. Human-Effigy Urn, ceramic, Weeden Island culture, Late Woodland period, A.D. 600–900 (cat. no. 64).

Plate 71. Charnel House Post with Eagle Effigy, wood (head restored), Belle Glade culture, Late Woodland period, A.D. 500–1000 (cat. no. 65).

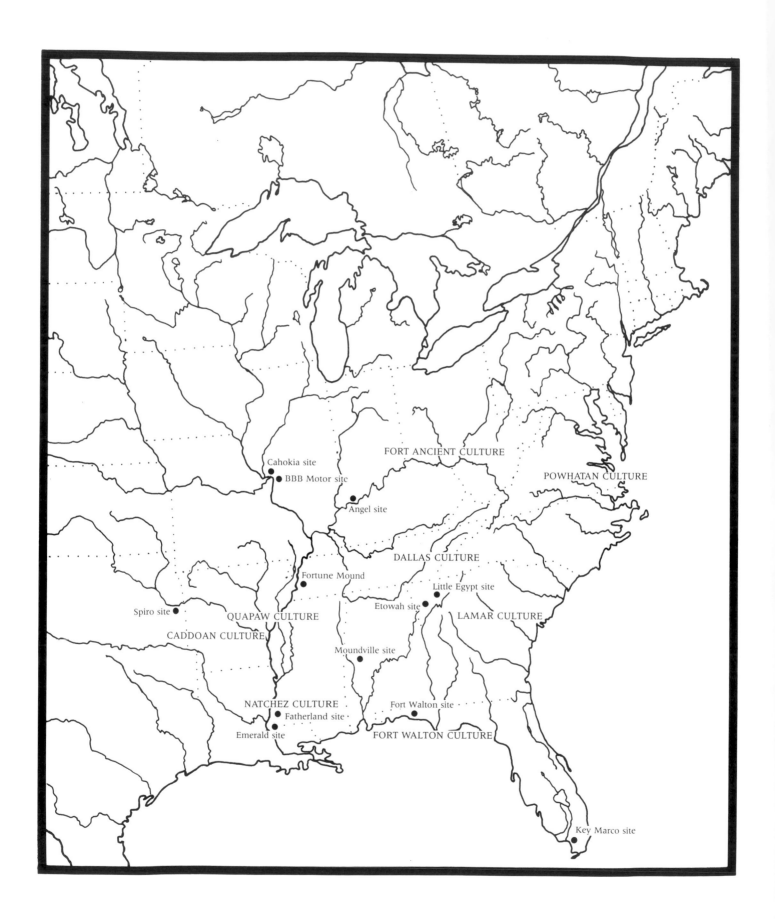

FORT ANCIENT CULTURE

POWHATAN CULTURE

Cahokia site
● BBB Motor site

●
Angel site

DALLAS CULTURE

Fortune Mound
●
Little Egypt site
●
Spiro site ●
QUAPAW CULTURE
Etowah site
●
LAMAR CULTURE

CADDOAN CULTURE

Moundville site
●

NATCHEZ CULTURE
Fort Walton site
●
● Fatherland site
Emerald site ●
FORT WALTON CULTURE

Key Marco site
●

III. THE MISSISSIPPIAN PERIOD

James A. Brown

Prehistoric art of the eastern Woodlands is one of the least studied areas of art in North America. Either tacked mechanically onto reviews of historic tribal arts or dismissed as a copy of Mesoamerican imagery, the art of the prehistoric Southeast, and particularly that of the late prehistoric, or Mississippian, period, has not been appreciated in its own right. There have been two principal barriers to proper appreciation of late prehistoric southeastern art. In the first place, the diversity of regional approaches has led, ironically, to a fragmented view of this art with meager recognition of its underlying organization. But, more devastatingly, the seeming parallels with Mesoamerican art have fostered the unsubstantiated notion that the imagery of the Southeast is derivative. As a consequence, the art work of the Mississippian period that is more polished and refined is dealt with infrequently on its own terms; the inspiration for this work is usually attributed, rather casually, to Mexico. It is too much to expect that entrenched wisdom will be dispelled by this or any other single essay, but it is my hope to lay the foundation for the eventual revision of prevailing views by sketching some fundamental premises concerning Mississippian-period imagery.

Between A.D. 1000 and 1600 a long period of stable cultures was established in the Southeast. The economic basis of most of these cultures was flood-plain agriculture, which provided stability to an economy that derived much of its food from hunting, fishing, and plant collection (Smith 1978). Corn was the major cultivated plant and—in combination with squash and beans—had become the basis for intensive agriculture by the end of the period. The amount of corn in the diet varied considerably within the Southeast. Those groups occupying western Arkansas and Oklahoma relied relatively little on corn (Perttula et al. 1982), while the economies of subtropical south Florida evidently did without it altogether (Goggin and Sturtevant 1964).

The dominant cultures of the Southeast were centered in the major river valleys, where large populations were supported by relatively intense agriculture (Smith 1978). In these valleys, large towns were established that provided a focus for political and ceremonial life (Morse and Morse 1983). These settlements dif-

Mississippian period sites and culture areas

93

fered greatly in size and compactness. The largest was the sprawling town of Cahokia, which is located in the broad alluvial bottom lands of the Mississippi River opposite St. Louis. This large town is unusual in its diffuse limits. Formal boundaries are indicated by four elongated marker mounds distinguished by ridged tops (Fowler 1969, 1978). These mounds form a diamond 3¼ by 2¼ miles that encloses an estimated 1,650 acres of mounds, plazas, habitations, and corn fields (Emerson 1982). Other well-known major towns are Citico, Emerald, Etowah, Harpeth (Mound Place), Moundville **(fig. 9)**, Parkin, and Spiro. They range in compactness from the large, three-hundred-acre stockaded town of Moundville to low-density towns which usually lack defensive earthworks (Peebles 1978; Steponaitis 1983). An example of the latter is the Spiro site cluster, which is a scattered series of settlements within a one- to two-square-mile area (J. A. Brown 1984).

A classic stockaded town of the period is Etowah, located on the banks of the river of the same name in northwestern Georgia **(fig. 10)**. This compact town of fifty-six acres is confined within a moatlike ditch (Thomas 1894; Moorehead 1932). The ditch was presumably part of defensive earthworks that surrounded the town on three sides, the remaining side being bounded by the river itself. Six mounds stood in the town within a layout of plazas and ordinary dwellings. Three of the mounds are massive earthworks. The largest, mound A **(fig. 11)**, standing sixty-one feet high and occupying a basal area of three acres, dominates the site (Thomas 1894). This large platform mound has a ramp projecting east into the plaza. To the south stand smaller platform mounds forming a small, shared courtyard. One of these, mound C, was a mortuary facility, from which the copper *Rogan Plates* **(fig. 12)** and stone mortuary figures came **(pls. 140,141)**. Investigation into this mound disclosed that burials were placed on the platform mound summit and in a ring of graves surrounding its foot (Larson 1971).

Platform Mounds and Their Uses

Large, flat-topped mounds were constructed in these towns to serve as the platforms of the major civic structures and the temple-shrines and residences of the elite. These mounds were laid out to carefully calculated specifications determined by sacred precepts known by the collective term of geomancy. The mounds were constructed in stages, sometimes over a considerable period of time. The larger ones were massive earthworks. The largest mound north of the Valley of Mexico is Monks mound, which is located near the center of the Cahokia town layout (Fowler 1974). This mound is 100 feet high and has a basal area of about

Figure 9. View of the Moundville site, Moundville, Alabama.

Plate 72. Bowl with Two Bird-Head Adornos (Fort Walton Incised), ceramic, Fort Walton culture, Late Mississippian period, A.D. 1350–1500 (cat. no. 66).

thirteen acres, which is approximately the size of the base of the Pyramid of Cheops in Egypt. But most mounds have modest elevations of ten feet or less. Even at Cahokia, over half of the estimated 120 mounds at the site are in this smaller size range.

Mounds and their associated plazas formed the nucleus of the civic and ceremonial life of the Mississippian-period communities. The most important ceremonial structures were the shrine houses, which usually stood on top of a major platform mound. These so-called "temples" were dedicated to the veneration of the ancestors of the elite and were the consecrated repositories of the tribe's sacred forces. A particularly clear instance of the use of the platform mound as the foundation of an ancestor-cult shrine is the "temple" of the historic Natchez, who were centered in the lower Mississippi valley. Archaeologists have shown that this temple must have occupied the summit of mound C of the Fatherland site (Neitzel 1965). A sacred fire was tended in this shrine that could not be allowed to go out without jeopardizing the fate of the tribe. A drawing was made of the shrine on the occasion of the 1725 funeral of Tattooed Serpent, the principal Natchez war chief and younger brother of the ruling Great Sun (Le Page Du Pratz 1758) **(fig. 13)**.

The senior member of the elite was typically the leader of the community. He derived much of his authority over the tribe from his embodiment of the sacred forces, which devolved to him through his descent from the solar deity via a line of past rulers.

The bones of these former rulers and their close relatives were housed in the shrine (Swanton 1911:166–174). The mounds continued to have ritual significance among some of the historic tribes until recently, long after platform mounds had ceased to be erected (Schnell et al. 1981). Such mounds were also used for elite residences. The use of mound B at the Fatherland site for this function is a typical case in point. This mound was located across the plaza from the temple mound C (Neitzel 1965).

The political use of ancestor shrines by rulers or chiefs of the more complexly organized tribes (technically, chiefdoms) in the early historic period was a culturally established means for extending centralized authority over their tribesmen. Temple shrines were the focal points of civil administration in several well-known chiefly societies of the historic period: the Calusa of Florida (Goggin and Sturtevant 1964), the Cofitachequi of Georgia (Garcilaso de la Vega 1951), the Natchez (Swanton 1911), and the Powhatan of Virginia (Swanton 1946). In these tribes the principal ancestor shrines were used as combined charnel houses and storehouses for objects of wealth and weaponry. In the Mississippian period, structures atop platform mounds were put to use in much the same way (J. A. Brown 1975). Wealth and weapons were interred with the dead in or near mortuary structures at Moundville in Alabama (mound C), Etowah in Georgia (mound C), and Spiro in Oklahoma (Craig mound) (Larson 1971; Peebles 1971; J. A. Brown 1975, 1976b).

The same pattern is present to a lesser degree in other major

Plate 73. Frog- or Fish-Effigy Bowl, ceramic, Fort Walton culture, Late Mississippian period, A.D. 1350–1500 (cat. no. 67).

centers (Hatch 1974). Since these associations recreate the essential features of the historic ancestor shrine, it is logical to suppose that the institution of such shrines had existed for a considerable time. Further, because these tribes were noteworthy for their degree of political centralization, it is reasonable to conclude that similar authority existed in the Mississippian period, from which richly furnished shrines have been found (Peebles and Kus 1977). Thus leaders during the prehistoric Mississippian era probably were effective in employing their religious authority to extend their military and economic power.

Style Regions in the Southeast

Analyses of the corpus of Mississippian art have disclosed an amazing diversity of styles, each—as we shall see—probably connected with a specific region (Muller 1966, 1979; Phillips and Brown 1978, 1983; J. A. Brown 1980). These styles are complex

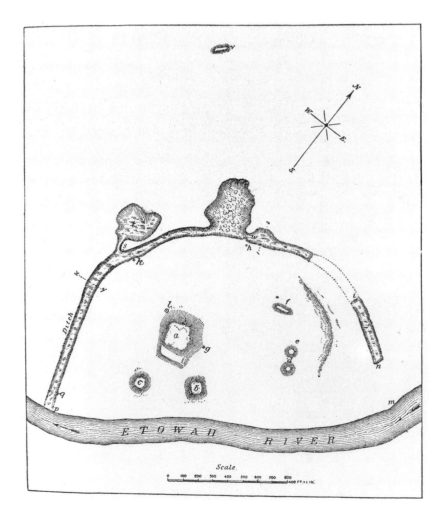

Figure 10. Plan of the Etowah group of earthworks prepared by Cyrus Thomas in 1885. Reproduced from Thomas 1894:299, fig. 182.

98

Figure 11. View of mound A, Etowah site, Cartersville, Georgia.

and developed according to varying principles. Most are realistic. Some emphasize a highly detailed, faithfully scaled reproduction of real objects, albeit in a distorted perspective reminiscent of ancient Egyptian art (pl. 117). Braden-style engraved shell objects, the red pipestone sculptures from Cahokia (pls. 110–114), and Etowah-style copper repoussé plates (fig. 12) are alike in this respect (Phillips and Brown 1978; Emerson 1982). The Craig style represents another, but very divergent, realistic approach to figural representation, specifically of warriors (Phillips and Brown 1978) (fig. 20).

Some very obscure images were created through strong conventionalization. Such designs as the conventionalized rattle-

Figure 12. *Rogan Plate* no. 1.
Etowah site, Bartow County,
Georgia. Reproduced from
Phillips and Brown 1978: fig.
268.

snake in the Citico style represent a late and very different working-out of the coiled rattlesnake theme (pl. 136) in the even later Scalloped Triskele (a three-legged figure) mode. In the latter example, the snake's neck and jaws have been reduced to centralized arcs placed around a small central "eye" and subordinated to the ring-shaped body coil (J. A. Brown 1983). The surrounding small circles, which probably represent a string of beads, are entirely extraneous. Differences in aesthetic canons can best be appreciated, however, by reference to differences in the manner in which the bird-man and related warrior themes were depicted in the Etowah copper style (fig. 12; pl. 117), the so-called "Mound C" style (pls. 133, 134), and the so-called "Spaghetti" style (Kneberg 1959; J. A. Brown 1983). The bird-man in the Spaghetti style (pl. 138) has been completely dissolved into a rhythmical intertwining of anatomical parts and costume to achieve an overall balance of body areas, lines, and perforations (Kneberg 1959).

The Craig style probably was connected with the Caddoan area (fig. 20; pls. 102–105); the Mound C style with the Dallas and Etowah cultures of the southern Appalachians (Phillips and Brown 1978) (fig. 19; pls. 133, 134); and the Scalloped Triskele style with the Tennessee-Cumberland cultural tradition centered around Nashville. The Spaghetti style may have been affiliated with the Floridian Gulf Coast (pls. 74, 124). Sculpture followed the same style boundaries as engraved and embossed objects. For example, Caddoan mortuary sculpture (pls. 95, 96) illustrates different principles from the figural sculpture of Etowah (pls. 140, 141). Tennessee-Cumberland mortuary figures are distinct from the latter two styles in their raised-leg posture (pl. 139).

Discussion of style regions inevitably leads to the subject of the so-called "pottery-style provinces." First developed by Holmes (1903), the configuration of pottery-style provinces has been considerably refined (Griffin 1967). Although similar to the style regions already discussed, pottery-style provinces are better defined in configuration. They include eastern Arkansas (pls. 82–85, 91, 92), the Caddoan area (pls. 76–80), Moundville (pl. 125), Tennessee-Cumberland (pl. 132), and Fort Walton in coastal Florida (pls. 72–74). Some of these modes are known to have had considerable longevity. For example, the Braden style of engraving had been established by A.D. 1100 (Phillips and Brown 1978). The related Moundville sub-style had begun by this time and continued until around A.D. 1500 (Steponaitis 1983).

Three major phases of thematic development can be tentatively identified in the Mississippian Southeast. The earliest was a "classic" phase (A.D. 1000–1300), when most of the iconic themes became established in their basic form. Some of the more

Figure 13. Mortuary ceremony for Tattooed Serpent. Reproduced from Le Page Du Pratz 1758, I:56.

representational figural work was created in this phase. Following it was an early "post-classic" phase (A.D. 1300–1500), during which representations of the human form were definitely less common **(pls. 102, 103, 125)**. The period between A.D. 1500 and 1700 saw a reduction in the diversity of imagery and a concentration on rattlesnake **(pl. 136)**, piasa (basically a panther with snake and bird characteristics, often with horns [Phillips and Brown 1978:140–143]), thunderbird, and death mask **(pl. 137)** motifs (Kneberg 1959).

Some of the more interesting documents of the classic phase are the massive pipes and figurines of brick-red pipestone resembling bauxite, the principal ore of aluminum. Many bear signature features that identify them as having come from the same workshop (Emerson 1982). The so-called *Big Boy* pipe from Spiro **(pl. 98)** and *Birger Figurine* **(pl. 113)**, both discussed below, are cases in point. These and other examples **(pl. 97)** were probably manufactured in the same region, possibly the Mississippi River valley heartland from Cahokia south to Memphis. Emerson (1982) has suggested that all of them were crafted originally as figurines, and that over time they were put to use as pipes to be smoked on ritual occasions. *Big Boy* is a good case in point because the stem hole was obviously bored through an already laid-out and carved, complicated relief pattern on the figure's cloak (J. A. Brown 1976b). The fact that this pipe was in use for a long time is indicated by its having been interred in a context dating around A.D. 1380, two hundred years after the *Birger Figurine—Big Boy's* contemporary—was buried (J. A. Brown 1984).

The imagery of the Mississippian period is extremely rich. A particularly large body of material is available from the corpus of engraved shell cups and gorgets (Phillips and Brown 1978, 1983). Important additions exist in engraved pottery and stone, repoussé copper, painted pottery, engraved bone, modeled pottery, and carved stone and wood (Fundaburk and Foreman 1957). As the stock of art work from dated contexts has accumulated, it has become increasingly apparent that the distinctive themes of the Mississippian period had become established by at least A.D. 1100 (J. A. Brown 1976a). Not only were they established early, but they were rendered in the distinct stylistic formats already discussed in connection with the different regions of the Southeast.

Mississippian Ancestor Cults

The ancestor shrine complexes of the Southeast exercised a decisive influence on the iconography of the Mississippian period. To appreciate this influence it is necessary to describe the relationship

Plate 74. Marine-Shell-Effigy Bowl (Pensacola Incised), ceramic, Fort Walton culture, Late Mississippian period, A.D. 1350–1500 (cat. no. 68).

of the cult of the ancestor shrine to two other major cult complexes, dominated respectively by the symbols of the falcon and the serpent. The corresponding fields of imagery are dominated by the skull, the falcon, and the serpent.

The concept of cult—a formalized set of rites dedicated to the veneration or propitiation of specific individuals, spirits, or forces—is a useful means for integrating the variety of themes and multiplicity of images and image combinations characteristic of Mississippian art. Quite a number of themes can be identified, but instead of simply recounting them, it seems more useful to organize them according to their primary cult affiliations. In his analysis of African cults, Turner (1974:185) drew a useful distinction between earth and fertility cults on the one hand and ancestral and political cults on the other. The former were observed to be socially inclusive, de-emphasizing the potentially sectarian interests of politics. In these cults, access to the relevant spirits is directly available to everyone and denied to no one. The politically manipulative cults, in contrast, are ones that typically emphasize some ultimate authority conferred exclusively upon a single individual or small group. Legitimacy of cult control is usually hereditary in these cases.

This distinction is particularly useful in relation to the functions of artifact, icon, and symbol in the art work of the Mississippian period. From a political perspective, the most important formally constituted cult in southeastern societies was that organized around the veneration of the ancestors of the elite. It had as its cult headquarters a house or shrine where cult paraphernalia was stored when not in use. Such shrines—for example, the Natchez temple discussed above (fig. 13)—were the repositories of the elite dead, generally in the form of a selection of cleaned and dried bones. Objects of wealth also were included: pearl beads, mica plates, and copper and marine-shell objects of all types. Of particular importance were larger objects such as copper ax heads and headdress plates and shell cups (Peebles 1971; J. A. Brown 1976a).

Each of the items deposited in the shrine houses was one that could readily be used for political purposes. The fetishes and ancestral bones represented the ultimate sacred relics. The coppers, pearls, and other sumptuary objects were tools for economic development and the means of making foreign alliances. Armaments held the potential for coercive action. These shrines assumed considerable importance in the social, economic, ritual, and political life of the community. They were treated in the early historic period with notable respect and fear inspired by the powerful supernatural forces that resided with the illustrious dead. As we have seen, the cult leader, as senior descendant of these dead, naturally derived considerable power through his embodiment of sacred forces, and the priests who helped him tend the shrine sometimes shared in the chief's elite status.

A basic furnishing of the shrine house was the ancestor cult figure. Sculpted in wood or stone, these images were evidently representations of the founding ancestor. Specific information in the form of contemporary observations is available about one such image, the wooden "idol" of the shrine of Powhatan, an early chief in Virginia (Swanton 1946) (fig. 14). Most shrines held one or more male figures (Black 1967; J. A. Brown 1975), but

Figure 14. John White, *Mortuary of Powhatan*, 1585–1587, watercolor. Reproduced from Lorant 1946:217.

104

Etowah and sites in north Georgia departed from this practice by equipping the shrine with pairs of male and female statuettes (Moorehead 1932; Larson 1971) (pl. 141). Whereas males presumably were considered to have been the founding ancestors in the Caddoan area of Spiro and in the Tennessee-Cumberland tribes, male and female couples were standard in the South.

The shrine figures were cared for scrupulously. One of them from Etowah (pl. 140) is supposed to have been found interred in its own box grave of limestone slabs (Moorehead 1932). Another (pl. 141), which is the male of a pair, was buried within a large tomb at the foot of the mound C ramp at the same site (Larson 1971). The figures had been broken during interment when they were dumped in a pit with a mixture of human bones and sumptuary items. This unusual treatment points to hasty and unceremonious burial. Since this grave was associated with a burnt rubbish layer originating up-slope on the mound—perhaps from destruction of the summit structure by fire—there is reason to infer that a major disaster befell the Etowans, including the distinct possibility of profanement due to a defeat similar to that of the Mississippi River Capaha as related in the 1541 narratives of Hernando de Soto. This account dramatically describes the ways in which the ancestor shrines were important to Indians of the area:

> ...the Casquins moved on to the temple in the large public plaza, which was the burial place of all who had ever ruled that land—the fathers, grandfathers and other ancestors of Capaha. The temples and sepulchres, as we have stated elsewhere, are the most venerated and esteemed sites among the natives of Florida [i.e., the Southeast]....Summoning all of their forces so that everyone might enjoy the triumph, the Casquins went to this temple and sepulchre, and since they realized how much Capaha...would resent their daring to enter and desecrate this place, they not only proceeded within but committed every infamy and affront they could. Sacking it of all ornaments and riches, they took the spoils and trophies which had been made from the losses of their own ancestors. Then they threw to the floor each of the wooden chests which served as sepulchres, and for their own satisfaction and vengeance as well as for an affront to their enemies, strewed upon the ground the very bones and bodies the chests enclosed. Afterward not content with having cast these remains to the ground, they trod upon them and kicked them with utter contempt and scorn (Garcilaso de la Vega 1951:438).

A fluorite figurine from the Angel site on the banks of the Ohio River was found in circumstances that shed light on the standard ritual treatment of these sacred mortuary images. It was discovered in a small pit dug into the southeast corner of the large platform of mound F (Black 1967). The type and size of structures above the uppermost construction layer are unknown because they had been completely eroded away. But beneath the upper mound stage was an earlier one with the well-preserved foundations of a large structure, forty-four by ninety feet in size (Black 1967). The maze of construction on this mound summit has the appearance of an interlocking complex of separate structures which were progressively more protected from outside access as one moved toward the south end. This architectural plan has all of the features usually associated with a place of extreme sanctity.

In tribes that lacked ancestor cults in historic times, other more condensed symbols of sacred ancestral power have been found. Carved shell masks (pl. 137), which were used as war magic among the historic Kansa of the eastern Plains, appear to have functioned as mortuary images in a simpler social setting (Howard 1956). They were used by the war chiefs of each clan as the object of mediation with the thunder or war god. The actual procedures as summarized by Skinner (1915) inform us that the historic use of shell masks and the war bundles in which they were kept recapitulated in a remarkable way the procedures the chiefs of the Mississippian period might have used to exercise their sacred powers to intercede for any suppliant. According to Skinner:

> On such an occurrence the relatives of the deceased would approach their gens [i.e., clan] bundle owner and give him a horse, bidding him to mourn from one to six months as the case might be.
>
> After this period had elapsed, the bundle owner would call the tribe to council and select four braves to help him as officers, gather a war party and set out. Before going into battle, the sacred bundle was opened and the two braves took from it the hawk or the sea shell [mask] and the reed and buckskin wrappers. The two warriors who did this thereby pledged themselves to kill an enemy or die in the attempt. These badges were hung around their necks by the leaders, who removed the charms at night before the party slept, and hung them on the forks of a crotched stick, whence they were removed and placed on their wearers early in the morning when they arose (1915:749).

From the importance conferred on face-mask gorgets, it is reasonable to infer similar functions for other imagery: the severed head and skull and bone symbols. These skeletal references harken back to the careful attention that most prehistoric societies conferred on the cleaning and curing of skulls and long bones of the honored dead.

Plate 75. Kneeling Feline Figure, wood, Calusa culture, Late Mississippian period, A.D. 1400–1500 (cat. no. 69).

The early historic literature contains numerous accounts of the curation of skeletal parts, and the sack of Capaha described above focuses on the symbolic effect that the destruction of the treasured bones of the elite had on the defeated tribe. The mortuary of Powhatan **(fig. 14)** contained bones of the elite in the chests pictured in the rear of the charnel house. The foresection housed the stacked, sand-filled "skins" of the same dead. The Natchez, too, practiced secondary burial. They disinterred the honored dead—including Tattooed Serpent **(fig. 13)**—after a period of earthen burial to allow for decomposition of the corpse (MacLeod 1982). The bones of these honored dead were finally interred in chests. Secondary burial for the tiny elite component of the population conformed to a well-known pattern of staged funeral ceremonies, in which mourning rites were enacted several times over a period of a year or more as the deceased became progressively less dangerous ideologically (Hertz 1960).

Although it may be appealing to propose an association between mortuary treatment and Mississippian "head pots" **(pls. 91–94)**, or skull and forearm-bone depictions **(pl. 124)**, a fundamental ambiguity surrounds them, especially the ceramic effigies of intact heads (J. A. Brown 1975; Phillips and Brown 1978). The frequency with which enemy trophy heads were collected and displayed implies the use of heads—and perhaps skulls—as symbols of military triumph. Tribal heads of the honored dead might easily have been mistaken for the trophy heads of the alien defeated. The account of the sack of Capaha is pertinent in this regard: "Many of the heads of Casquin Indians which the men of Capaha had placed on the points of lances at the doors of the temple as a symbol of victory and triumph, they now removed, substituting for them the heads of citizens of the town whom they themselves had decapitated on that very day" (Garcilaso de la Vega 1951:438–439).

The symbolic uses of heads, particularly actual severed heads, as trophies mandate caution in interpreting isolated head designs in Mississippian art. This caution does not necessarily extend to skull and bone motifs, which are more likely to denote ancestor veneration because of the care implied by the cleaned bones that is absent in the case of severed heads.

The Iconography of Chiefs

Chiefly iconography was expressed during the Mississippian period by three major themes: the chiefly litter, the player of chunkey, a game involving a stone roller and throwing sticks, and the falcon impersonator. Tying these themes to representations of tribal

Figure 15. Gorget showing
litter motif, woodpecker
heads, and circle-and-cross
motif, marine shell. Mississippi. Reproduced from Holmes
1883: pl. 58.

political leaders is the ubiquitous presence of certain key emblems of office, the columella pendant (a pendant fashioned from the core of a conch or whelk shell) and the bellows- or heart-shaped apron. The chiefly litter motif consists basically of the framework of a litter enclosing a cross-in-circle design (J. A. Brown 1983). A variation has woodpecker heads drawn perpendicular to the sides **(fig. 15)**, and, in one pictorial image in the Craig style, a warrior chief is depicted rising from the litter and grasping severed heads in both hands. The litter constitutes a reference to a mode of transport that was specific to the office of the central political leader in many of the tribal societies of the historic Southeast (Swanton 1911, 1946) **(fig. 16)**. Litters, which only rarely have been preserved in prehistoric contexts, have a history going back to at least A.D. 1100, the date of the Cahokian examples from mound 72 (Fowler 1969, 1974) **(fig. 17)**. The cross-in-circle design conveys, among other meanings, the solar deity as embodied in the chief. In combining symbolically the sources of sacred authority and military might, the litter motif represents one of the more condensed symbolic statements of chiefly authority.

The chunkey-player theme conveys a more pictorial message. The figure is usually shown grasping the stone roller, or dis-

Opposite:
Plate 76. Engraved Bottle (Haley Engraved), ceramic, Haley phase, Caddoan culture, Mississippian period, A.D. 1200–1400 (cat. no. 70).

Left:
Plate 77. Double Bottle (Hudson Engraved), ceramic, Caddoan culture, Late Mississippian period, A.D. 1500–1800 (cat. no. 71).

111

coidal, and stripped-stick gaming pieces. In some depictions the player's costume includes an elaborate looped belt and spool-shaped hat (**fig. 18**). A Mississippian-period pipe (**pl. 97**) depicts a chunkey player, without his official costume, holding a discoidal in his right hand and two game sticks in his left.

The importance of the chunkey-player role transcended both the recreational aspect of the game itself and the way in which it is represented in descriptions from historic times, when it was played among Muskogean-speaking peoples and their neighbors in the deep South. The stone discoidals were carefully kept in the towns to which they belonged (Swanton 1946:547). The game's basic features have been described this way: "The essence of the game was to start the [stone] roller along a smooth piece of

Figure 16. The Natchez chief Great Sun transported on a litter. Reproduced from Le Page Du Pratz 1758, II:368.

ground with which every town was supplied, after which the two players threw their poles after it with the idea of hitting the stone, coming as near it as possible when the stone came to rest, or preventing the opponents from accomplishing either of these results" (Swanton 1946:682).

The chunkey-player's role appears to have been associated originally with divination. The basis for this inference is the Cherokee myth of Wild Boy (Mooney 1900:246). In the course of his search for his father, Wild Boy used a "gaming wheel" to determine the correct direction in which he should travel. In the myth this direction was found after the wheel failed to return (magically) upon a roll. On this basis it is reasonable to postulate that the configuration in which a stripped pole and chunkey stone landed with respect to each other would have been fruitful material for "reading," much as tea leaves are "read" today.

112

The third significant motif of chiefly iconography is the falcon impersonator, who is shown brandishing a club and carrying a severed head (J. A. Brown 1975, 1976a) (fig. 19). The bird-man theme refers to a cult complex in its own right. The costume particular to this role consisted of a hawk-wing cape, forked-eye markings, and a raptorial bird beak (figs. 20, 21). The connotations of the falcon impersonator include fighting and warfare (J. A. Brown 1976a). Although the various depictions of elite roles usually do not occur together, an exception is the *Mangum Plate*, which shows a figure in combined chunkey-player and falcon-impersonator costume (Phillips and Brown 1978:205) (fig. 21). The chunkey player's connection with the falcon imperson-

Figure 17. Excavated remains of wooden litters. Mound 72, Cahokia site, St. Clair County, Illinois. Photo: James A. Brown.

Figure 18. Gorget showing a chunkey player, marine shell. Perry County, Missouri. Mississippian period, A.D. 1250–1450. Reproduced from Mac-Curdy 1913: pl. 49.

ator on this object confirms the political significance of the chunkey-player role.

A major military cult involved the widespread depiction of falcons and falconid eye (forked-eye) markings and the common use of weapon-derived badges of status in intimate association with falcon dress. In its basic form the falcon occurs as a flattened-out bird viewed from the front or back. Present are the distinctive ventral spots, albeit exaggerated, barred wing feathers, and facial markings reminiscent of the forked eye, all of which leave no doubt as to the species (Byers 1962; J. A. Brown 1975, 1976b) **(fig. 22)**. Curiously, this classic image has the appearance of a dead bird, an attitude at variance with the falcon's aerial boldness in knocking its prey to earth with the force of its powerful dives. The most common objects on which the falcon appears are repoussé copper plates **(pls. 117–120)**, which were designed either to be worn on the front of headdresses or to be tied to long hairpins standing upright in the hair (Hamilton et al. 1974). The humanization of these and other animals is characteristic of Mississippian art. Falcons are shown bedecked with necklaces and other artifacts and are sometimes depicted with human heads and other body parts. These substitutions show an attempt to car-

114

Figure 19. Gorget showing a falcon-man, marine shell. Mississippian period, A.D. 1200–1450. Photo: The Museum of the American Indian, Heye Foundation, New York.

ry through the falcon identity of the warrior by incorporating a falconid beak, eye markings, and feather-like "hair" at the back of the neck **(pl. 117)**.

The most complete expression of the Mississippian warrior theme is embodied in the falcon-impersonator image already mentioned (Phillips and Brown 1978:124–130). This theme was expressed in the broadest range of styles. In it a human warrior in falcon costume strikes a warlike pose. This theme was made famous by the finding of the graceful copper *Rogan Plates* at Etowah in the last century (Thomas 1894). On the more complete of these plates **(fig. 12)** the warrior brandishes a mace in his right hand and grasps a "severed head"—either a rattle shaped like a head or the real thing—in his left hand. Other media, such as engraved shell cups and gorgets **(pls. 133, 134)**, display variations on this theme. Falcon impersonators are shown wearing different types of elaborate headdresses that incorporate one or more of the caps, plates, feathers, and animal pelts commonly worn by warriors (Phillips and Brown 1978). Completing the warrior's dress is a stiffened forelock of hair with a large shell bead tied to its base.

The famous *Big Boy* pipe **(pl. 98)** from Spiro discussed above reveals details of costume that are not readily apparent in the two-

Figure 20. Engraving of a falcon-man on a marine-shell cup. Craig mound, Spiro site, Le Flore County, Oklahoma. Mississippian period, A.D. 1200–1350. Photo: James A. Brown.

Figure 21. *Mangum Plate* no. 1. Mangum site, Clairborne County, Mississippi. Mississippian period, A.D. 1200–1400. Reproduced from Phillips and Brown 1978: fig. 268.

Figure 22. Peregrine falcon *(falco peregrinus)*. Photo: James A. Brown.

dimensional images. The cap consists of a flat tablet held at a tilt by a strap around the figure's hair, which is worn in a bun. This tablet appears to contain a copper plate (decorated with an ogee, or double-curve, symbol) that is a common type found in the graves of the Mississippian elite (Hamilton et al. 1974). Accompanying the figure's very simple dress are a rope of bead necklaces in front, a long, thick braid of hair at the side, and a cloak, decorated with feather symbols, which undoubtedly represents a wing cape (J. A. Brown 1976b). Ear ornaments are maskettes of the so-called "long-nosed-god" type (pl. 115).

Actual confirmation of the existence of these elements of costume is forthcoming from several sites. The grave furnishings of one elite Etowan burial from Mound C (Larson 1971) included a large headdress plate resting on the deceased's brow; another copper ornament rested close by, where a separate hair ornament could be expected. An example of a square head plaque (pl. 116) was found next to the skull of a stone box burial (Thomas 1894). Presumably it had been mounted in the fashion of the headdress on the *Rogan Plate*. In the same grave was a discoidal and—appar-

Plate 78. Bottle (Baily Engraved), ceramic, Caddoan culture, Mississippian period, A.D. 1200–1500 (cat. no. 72).

Plate 79. Tripod Bottle (Hodges Engraved), ceramic, Caddoan culture, Mississippian period, A.D. 1200–1500 (cat. no. 73).

118

Left:
Plate 80. Seed Jar, ceramic, Caddoan culture, Late Mississippian period, A.D. 1300–1500 (cat. no. 74).

Opposite:
Plate 81. Bottle (Nashville Negative Painted), ceramic, Mississippian period, A.D. 1300–1500 (cat. no. 75).

ently—another falcon plate in the style of the *Wulfing Plates* found in southeastern Missouri. Woven cloaks with feather markings that could have been the "wings" of the falcon impersonator are known from other sites (J. A. Brown 1975) **(fig. 23)**. The clubs represented in art refer either to maces or ceremonial axes (J. A. Brown 1975); some of the latter, carved from a single block of stone, are known as monolithic axes **(pls. 99, 100)**. These were obviously non-functional, but were hypertrophic renditions of real objects meant to be understood as emblems of rank in societies that conferred status on the basis of individual exploits.

The ear ornaments worn by falcon impersonators include the long-nosed-god maskettes already mentioned (Williams and Goggin 1956; Bareis and Gardener 1968; Harn 1974; Anderson 1975). These charming ornaments **(pl. 115)** of marine shell or copper are remarkably uniform, shield-shaped maskettes with a double, squared-off crown, circular eyes, and a large nose of varying length (Williams and Goggin 1956). The more elaborate ones possess long noses that are either wavy or straight. Widely distributed during the classic phase of artistic development (A.D. 1000–1300), they held symbolic associations that are obscure today, partly because this type of ear ornament passed from use by the end of that phase. In a recent discussion of these images (Hall 1983), it was pointed out that these little heads recall the description of the Siouan mythic figure Red Horn, who was known as "He-who-wears-human-heads-as-earrings."

It must be noted in connection with the iconography of the falcon that this bird—or hawks of any type—should not be confused with the eagle. These two raptors were kept quite separate iconographically in Mississippian art, at least during the classic phase. Eagles, unlike the more delicately boned falcons, were depicted with large, raptorial beaks on the same scale as their heads. In addition, their head feathers were rendered as shaggy in Caddoan art of the Craig school, i.e., in a manner identical to the handling of buffalo coats (Phillips and Brown 1983).

The Serpent and Fertility Cults

On its most inclusive level, the Mississippian earth cult was appropriately connected with images of fertility. One of the most symbolic of the artifacts available to us is the *Birger Figurine* mentioned earlier **(pl. 113)**, which came from a small satellite site of Cahokia (Emerson 1982). This statuette depicts a woman "cultivating" the back of a serpent with a hoe. The serpent is not an ordinary snake. It is monstrous, with a catlike head showing the

Figure 23. Fragments of a woven cloth with feather designs. Craig mound, Spiro site, Le Flore County, Oklahoma. Mississippian period, A.D. 1200–1350. Photo: The Museum of the American Indian, Heye Foundation, New York.

Plate 82. Bottle with Spiral Design (Nodena Red and White), ceramic, Late Mississippian period, A.D. 1300–1500 (cat. no. 76).

Plate 83. Bottle with Spiral Design (Nodena Red and White), ceramic, Late Mississippian period, A.D. 1300–1500 (cat. no. 77).

distinctive non-ophidian eyes, muzzle, and dentition of a panther or other felid (Emerson 1982). Since it has no horns, strictly speaking it cannot be termed a piasa. Gourd-bearing vines grow from the serpent's body behind the place where the cultivator's hoe has dug into it.

This statuette represents a story, recounted in stone, of the dynamic process of conversion of the serpent's body into human sustenance. One of the striking features of this graphic portrayal is that the panther-serpent's gift is not corn—the staple of the Mississippian diet—but a plant of more ancient status as a domesticate in the American Midwest. Botanists have suggested that the yellow-flowered gourd (*Cucurbita pepo, ovifera* species) is depicted here (Emerson 1982). Descendants of this species were among the earliest cultivated plants in the eastern United States (Conard et al. 1984). Originally the seeds were probably the object of cultivation. Subsequent selection for fleshy fruit led to the modern pumpkin and related squashes. The agricultural message conveyed by the gift of gourd food is reinforced by the burden basket carried on the cultivator's back.

Distinctive burden baskets have been found consistently with female (non-mortuary) figurines in which the collection and processing of grain or seed foods are emphasized. Although not many images of women have survived in Mississippian-period art, the few statuettes and pipes that exist feature the grinding of grain on a grinding stone (Emerson 1982:8–10) **(pl. 114)** or in a mortar (Burnett 1945:12–13, pls. 7–9; Emerson 1982:15–16). Each of these figurines has a "back-pack" burden basket.

The gourd-giving serpent of the *Birger Figurine* forms a bridge between agricultural symbolism and the imagery of serpents and panthers. In fact, serpents occur in such proliferation and with such variation in Mississippian art that it is not surprising that they connect with the most inclusive of the Mississippian-period cults. The basic depiction is of a simple rattlesnake; one of the more fanciful is a pair of double-headed snakes shown knotted together. A single-headed and horned version is depicted on a paint palette from Moundville **(pl. 121)**. The knotting together of a pair of snakes recalls the crown of snakes and blue-jay feathers made by the Corn Mother for her hero son in Creek myth (Witthoft 1949:78–79). This mythic association of a snake headdress with the corn-giver brings us back to the theme represented by the *Birger Figurine*. Saurian images such as the frog **(pls. 78, 110)**, lizard, and turtle **(pls. 84, 89)** would logically occupy approximately the same position as the serpent in Mississippian iconography.

As important as the serpent was, it does not monopolize Mississippian fertility symbolism. The panther or puma is also an important symbol whose status is confirmed by the peculiar piasa. A similar creature is often described simply as a "winged rattle-snake" (pl. 125). The identification of the piasa as an image type occurred as a result of an episode involving Father Jacques Marquette that occurred on the banks of the Mississippi between the mouths of the Illinois and Missouri rivers during the early seventeenth century. After having been warned that there were monsters in the Mississippi, Marquette recounted the following:

> While Skirting some rocks, which by Their height and Length inspired awe, We saw upon one of them two painted monsters which at first made Us afraid, and upon Which the boldest savages dare not Long rest their eyes. They [the monsters] are large As a calf; they have Horns on their heads Like those of deer, a horrible look, red eyes, a beard Like a tiger's, a face somewhat like a man's, a body Covered with scales, and so Long A tail that it winds all around the Body, passing above the head and going back between the legs, ending in a Fish's tail (Thwaites 1896–1901, LIX:139–141).

The truth of this account has been a subject of controversy, starting as early as 1687 when other voyagers down the Mississippi failed to relocate this painting. Time may have obliterated its traces, but the *idea* of the piasa painting did not go away. Evidently others appeared in the same place a century later. These inspired a small industry of pictures (Madden 1974) and accounts that do not stand up to historical criticism (Temple 1956). The nearby stream became known as Piasa Creek. However fanciful some of these accounts may seem, it is amazing how well they accord with a specific prehistoric image and with depictions of the dreaded Underwater Panther, which has retained its mythic form to this day among Great Lakes Indians. Its role in Native American symbolism of the Great Lakes area points to the same fertility connection.

An excellent example of the panther as piasa is a shell cup fragment (pl. 103). In this instance the basically feline body is marked off horizontally into mammalian and reptilian coats, with scales on top and circles on the bottom. An avian feather-like element was added down the spine. The bird talons were humanized by shell-bead "anklets." This cup closely resembles depictions of the Underwater Panther (J. H. Howard 1968).

The piasa theme is represented by other examples. Cat heads mounted on rattlesnake bodies are arranged in a swastika around a cross-in-circle element (pl. 102). Ceramic vessels contain panther/piasa effigy heads and tails. Simple depictions of panthers without the piasa associations are represented by a pipe from the lower Mississippi valley (pl. 130) and by a unique, small fetish

Plate 84. Turtle-Effigy Vessel (Avenue Polychrome), ceramic, Quapaw culture, Late Mississippian period, A.D. 1300–1500 (cat. no. 78).

Plate 85. Dog-Effigy Vessel, ceramic, Late Mississippian period, A.D. 1500 (cat. no. 79).

Plate 86. Bowl with Crested-Bird Adorno (Leland Incised), ceramic, Late Mississippian period, A.D. 1300–1500 (cat. no. 80).

figurine from the Calusa area of south Florida (Goggin and Sturtevant 1964) **(pl. 75)**.

The many abstract motifs of scrolls, whorls, and undulating elements seen in Mississippian art probably also connect with the fertility cult. Their very common deployment on pottery **(pls. 85, 86)** and other items receiving broad use in the community attests to the possibility of a connection, even of a distant type, to this most popular of cults.

The Serpent and the Skull

Two antithetical social forces were at work in Mississippian societies: autonomy versus centralized political autocracy. The interests and aspirations of each were represented by the fertility cults of the populace on the one hand and the ancestor cults organized by the elite on the other. Standing, as it were, with a leg in each camp was the military cult of the falcon, which probably commanded the allegiance of major segments of the masses, but was firmly under the control of the elite.

Plate 87. Frog-Effigy Vessel
(Bell Plain), ceramic, Mississippian period, A.D. 1200–
1500 (cat. no. 81).

130

Plate 88. Bear-Effigy Bottle,
ceramic, Mississippian period,
A.D. 1200–1500 (cat. no. 82).

Plate 89. Turtle-Effigy Vessel
(Bell Plain), ceramic, Late
Mississippian period, A.D.
1300–1500 (cat. no. 83).

Overleaf:
Plate 91. Human-Head-Effigy Vessel (Nodena Red and White), ceramic, Late Mississippian period, A.D. 1300–1500 (cat. no. 85).

Plate 92. Human-Head-Effigy Vessel (Nodena Red and White), ceramic, Late Mississippian period, A.D. 1300–1500 (cat. no. 86).

Plate 90. Reclining-Human-Effigy Bowl, ceramic, Late Mississippian period, A.D. 1300–1500 (cat. no. 84).

Plate 93. Human-Head-Effigy
Vessel, ceramic, Late Mississippian period, A.D. 1300–
1500 (cat. no. 87).

Plate 94. Human-Head-Effigy,
red cedar, Spiro phase, Caddoan culture, Mississippian
period, A.D. 1200–1350
(cat. no. 88).

Plate 95. Seated Male Figurine, wood, Spiro phase, Caddoan culture, Mississippian
period, A.D. 1200–1350
(cat. no. 89).

Plate 96. Seated Male Figurine, wood and pigment, Spiro phase, Caddoan culture, Mississippian period, A.D. 1200–1350 (cat. no. 90).

Plate 97. Chunkey-Player-Effigy Pipe, bauxite, Caddoan culture, Mississippian period, A.D. 1200–1350 (cat. no. 91).

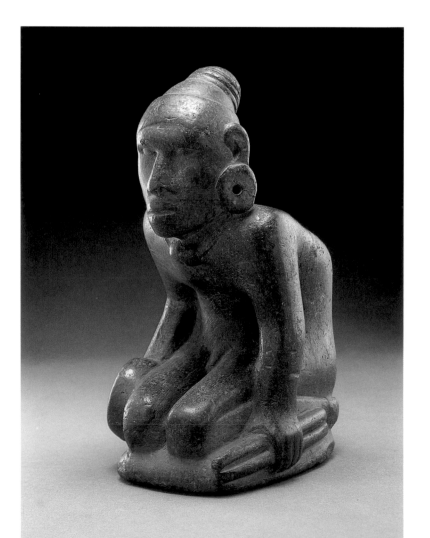

Opposite:
Plate 98. *Big Boy* (Effigy Pipe), bauxite, Spiro phase, Caddoan culture, Mississippian period, A.D. 1200–1350 (cat. no. 92).

We know much more about popular, household beliefs among Mississippian peoples than about those controlled by the elite. The persistence of popular cults and the beliefs of the non-elite among historic-period tribes is a fruitful avenue of inquiry. This persistence stands in marked contrast to the lack of same evidenced by the ancestor and falcon cults. In fact the practices of a few tribes in early historic times are our sole record of ancestor cults (Waring 1968). The falcon cult has completely disappeared, and its memory has been so obliterated that early scholars tried their utmost—incorrectly, as we have shown—to interpret the falcon images uncovered archaeologically as eagles, whether spotted or plain (Spinden 1913; Willoughby 1932; Waring and Holder 1945).

Now that the basis for Mississippian-period art has been described in terms of the political approaches to social and economic realities in small-scale societies, it should be apparent that forces were at work outside Mesoamerica that dictated the imagery and vehicles for artistic creation in the Southeast. Of paramount importance is the conclusion that many classic-period works sprang from the tensions between the elite-controlled sacred cults and the popular belief systems grounded in fertility spirits. Out of this dynamic interplay emerged the military cults, which provided a social bridge between the honors and privileges of the elite and the masses of rank-and-file farmers. The very ubiquity of the symbolism associated with the military cults signifies that it was part of the means for social advancement among the populace. In this sense the widespread use of falcon symbolism became the iconography of a social movement. Balanced against this were the exclusive ancestor cult images of the skull and bones of the elite. The serpent, the panther, and the imagery connected with the fertility cults, presumably having had ancient roots common to every household, retained broad support throughout the Mississippian period.

Plate 99. Monolithic Ax, stone, Spiro phase, Caddoan culture, Mississippian period, A.D. 1200–1350 (cat. no. 93).

Plate 100. Monolithic Ax, stone, Spiro phase, Caddoan culture, Mississippian period, A.D. 1200–1350 (cat. no. 94).

Opposite:
Plate 101. Repoussé Male
Profile, copper, Spiro phase,
Caddoan culture, Mississippi-
an period, A.D. 1200–1350
(cat. no. 95).

Plate 102. Engraved Shell
Cup Showing Four Horned
Serpents, marine shell, Spiro
phase, Caddoan culture, Mississippian period, A.D. 1200–
1350 (cat. no. 96).

Plate 103. Engraved Cup Fragment, marine shell, Spiro phase, Caddoan culture, Mississippian period, A.D. 1200–1350 (cat. no. 97).

Plate 104. Bird-Head Effigy, marine shell, Spiro phase, Caddoan culture, Mississippian period, A.D. 1200–1350 (cat. no. 98).

Plate 105. Engraved Pendant
Showing a Pair of Hands,
marine shell, Spiro phase,
Caddoan culture, Mississippian period, A.D. 1200–1350
(cat. no. 99).

IV. CONTINUITIES OF IMAGERY AND SYMBOLISM IN THE ART OF THE WOODLANDS

David W. Penney

Exchange and the Primitive Valuable

The manufacturing and distribution of art participate in a wide range of other social processes and motives with which art works become identified. It may seem obvious to point out that the meticulously crafted art work represents a value that can be transferred in exchange for services, profit, or increased social influence. Whereas the modern world understands value in economic terms—those of purchase, barter, and trade—the exchange of valued objects in many preliterate societies served a related, but slightly different, social purpose. It created and maintained crucial obligations among individuals, families, clans, and communities.

Many art works from the ancient Woodlands apparently functioned as "primitive valuables," objects circulated among individuals and groups via extensive exchange networks of trading partners. Trade relationships resulted in certain kinds of advantages for a social group. As Brose (1979b) has shown, trade partnerships became advantageous when societies suffered from occasional shortfalls in locally available food supplies. We have seen how the growth of populations restricted to specific territories during the Late Archaic period (3000–1000 B.C.), coupled with slowly changing climatic conditions, made it necessary for communities to seek insurance, i.e., a friendly neighboring group which might share in times of need. Trade relationships, probably linked with intermarriage, created these mutually beneficial social bonds.

Trade also played an extremely important role in the process of internal social ordering within Late Archaic and Woodland societies. So far as can be understood on the basis of the archaeological evidence, all of the societies of these early periods of Woodlands history operated as simply structured, egalitarian bands. As in some of the societies of historic-period Native Americans, leadership status was determined only by an individual's ability to influence others. In recent Native American societies, there were several traditionally sanctioned ways for an individual to gain influence: eloquence (the ability to convince others through dialogue); physical strength and bravery (usually not

Plate 106. Nursing-Mother-Effigy Bottle, ceramic, Mississippian period, A.D. 1200–1400 (cat. no. 100).

manifested through coercion, but demonstrated instead in socially accepted ways so that others would acquiesce through the acknowledgment of courageous and important deeds); and the distribution of wealth.

A wealthy individual did not "purchase" agreement with his point of view. With generous gifts, acquisition of ceremonial rights, and the sponsorship of others, a wealthy man gained influence and, ultimately, political power. Trade in primitive valuables offered the opportunity to achieve wealth and social influence to those who were especially adept at manipulating the exchange networks, thus maintaining and expanding the number of trade partners as well as a wise distribution of valuables within their own groups. Often the family or clan acted as a corporate unit in order to advance the social position of all. This resulted in a number of advantages: choice of marriage partners, better access to resources, more and firmer alliances with other groups, and so on.

Much of what circulated through the Woodlands exchange networks was valuable raw material, most importantly marine shell and copper. Marine shell, collected from the southern Atlantic coast and the Gulf of Mexico, was in great demand among Woodlands traders for many centuries. Throughout the South and as far north as Wisconsin, Michigan, and Ontario, Late Archaic peoples fashioned marine shell into a great variety of ornaments, pendants, and gorgets (pl. 21). Most Late Archaic copper—which, as we have seen, circulated throughout central and northeastern North America—rarely moved further south than Kentucky and Tennessee. It was transformed into beads, ornaments, and various kinds of tools (pls. 13–15). Native North American technology did not include smelting and casting; copper was shaped by cold hammering, annealing, cutting, and grinding.

As has been mentioned, the expansive trade networks of the Middle Woodland period (200 B.C.–A.D. 500) increased the quantities of copper and marine shell circulating through the Woodlands region. Copper plates, celts of various sizes (fig. 24), ornaments, panpipes, and effigy cutouts (fig. 25) were made by several regional groups during this period, including those of the Southeast and Gulf Coast (pls. 37–40). Large conch-shell (often the *busycon* genus) cups and enormous quantities of marine-shell beads were imported to the Midwest. The Ohio Hopewell collected marine shell and copper in unparalleled quantities; thousands of copper and marine-shell objects were recovered from the major Ohio centers of Mound City, Hopewell, Seip, and elsewhere.

Copper and marine-shell objects became associated with the highest-status individuals of the Mississippian period (A.D. 1000–1600) and often, as we have seen, possessed elaborate religious

Figure 24. Pair of celts, copper. Seip site, Ross County, Ohio. Middle Woodland period, A.D. 1–400. Photo: Ohio Historical Society, Columbus.

iconography. The Mississippian mortuary centers in Spiro, Etowah, and elsewhere contained vast numbers of carved or engraved marine-shell containers and circular gorgets and copper plaques worked in repoussé, all conveying rich information about Mississippian ritual and cosmology **(pls. 101–105, 115–120, 133, 137, 138)**. Trade in copper and shell continued throughout the Woodlands until the time of European discovery (Cabeza de Vaca 1904: 74–75; J. Howard 1953; Fogel 1963; Goad 1978).

Copper and shell, then, represented considerable value throughout the history of the Woodlands region. The materials were difficult to obtain and possessed physical properties that must have increased their value to Native peoples who lived far away from their sources. The spiritual substance of these materials was of even greater significance, however, as evidenced by their importance to most historic tribes. Among the most sacred objects of the Creeks, for example, are a group of copper plates that accompanied the tribe on their long trek westward to Oklahoma during the early nineteenth century (Swanton 1928:503–510). Copper nuggets appear in Great Lakes sacred bundles **(fig. 26)**. Copper is believed to be a powerful spiritual substance derived from the underworld, and a marine shell known as the *megis* is considered to be the pivotal religious object of the Grand Medicine Lodge, or Midéwiwin, religion of several Great Lakes tribes (Densmore 1929:86–95).

Many objects in finished form circulated through the exchange networks as well. Most fall into two basic categories: ornaments, such as beads, pendants, gorgets **(pls. 20, 21)**,

149

Figure 25. Eagle effigy, copper. Hopewell site, Ross County, Ohio. Middle Woodland period, 200 B.C.–A.D. 400. Photo: Field Museum of Natural History, Chicago.

Figure 26. *Sacred Bundle* containing a copper effigy, twined fiber and copper, (bag) l. 19.4 cm, (effigy) l. 14.2 cm. Winnebago people, nineteenth century. The Detroit Institute of Arts, Founders Society Purchase.

breastplates, and so on, and tools or implements. The exchange of implements does not appear to have been motivated by an interest in their utilitarian applications, however. The material and workmanship of these special tools display their makers' great interest in the aesthetic qualities of the objects. Many show no signs of wear or were made in such a way as to have been practically useless; these include long, gracefully shaped, inordinately thin blades with eccentrically shaped bases **(figs. 3, 27)**. The materials often came from faraway sources and exhibit especially attractive visual qualities. These objects were clearly the subject of high aesthetic regard and may have been thought of as effigies of tools rather than as utilitarian objects, as we shall see.

Copper knives, blades, and points from the Late Archaic Old Copper complex of Wisconsin, Michigan, and Ontario were made in several styles displaying formal qualities of great aesthetic refinement **(pls. 13–15)**. Archaeologists have debated whether these beaten copper tools were "technomic" or "ideotechnic," i.e., whether they were technically efficient or perhaps more socially motivated status objects (Binford 1971; McHugh 1973). The functional efficacy of Old Copper tools can legitimately be questioned, while abundant evidence exists for the special regard in which they were held as high-status burial offerings. An Old Copper burial discovered on the bluffs overlooking Lake Superior in Michigan contained a collection of enormous Old Copper tools, a socketed blade **(pl. 13)**, a large knife **(pl. 14)**, and other objects whose proportions negate their usefulness as tools or weapons. Their social importance resided in the amount of valuable raw material from which they were made and in their visual impressiveness. It may be appropriate to regard Old Copper tools of this type in the same way that European cultures have regarded comparable objects made of gold and other precious materials: as valuable and beautiful, but not for mundane use.

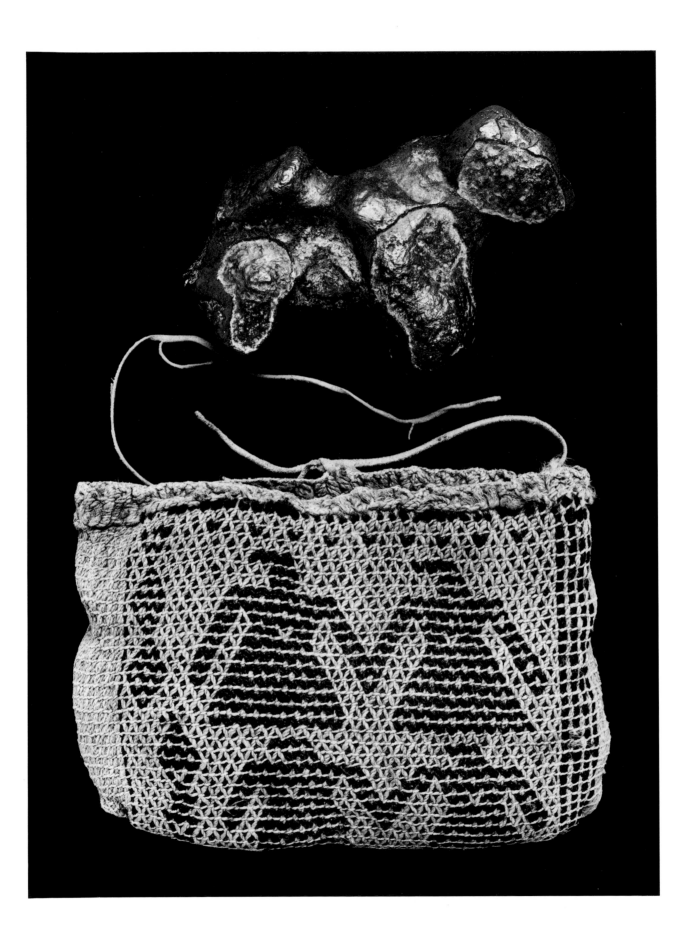

The concept of the "sumptuary implement," a tool effigy made of valuable and attractive materials, dominated art-making of the Late Archaic period and continued as an important aspect of Woodlands culture through the Mississippian period. The Late Archaic turkey-tail points already mentioned—large, leaf-shaped blades, carefully made and distinctively shaped with pointed bases—were traded throughout the central and Great Lakes Woodlands **(fig. 3)**. Made of high-quality Harrison County flint and much too delicate for use, they accompany many high-status

Figure 27. Pair of blades, obsidian. Hopewell site, Ross County, Ohio. Middle Woodland period, 200 B.C.–A.D. 400. Photo: Field Museum of Natural History, Chicago.

burials of the Red Ocher traditon (Didier 1967). Enormous, eccentrically shaped blades made of obsidian collected from the Yellowstone valley in Colorado became important, high-status symbols for the Ohio Hopewell of the Middle Woodland period **(fig. 27)**. A great deal of copper was traded during the Middle Woodland period in the form of simple, rectangular ax blades which show no signs of wear **(fig. 24)**. Monolithic axes, stone sculptures of axes hafted on wooden handles **(pls. 99, 100)**, were made for the Mississippian elite at Spiro, Moundville, Etowah, and other Mississippian centers. None of these objects possessed any usefulness beyond conveying the status or wealth of their owners.

Bannerstones **(pls. 1–12)**, in their more elaborate forms, may also be considered as a kind of sumptuary implement. A bannerstone functioned as part of an *atlatl*, or spear-thrower, a rod with a

Plate 107. Kneeling-Human-Effigy Bottle (Bell Plain), ceramic, Late Mississippian period, A.D. 1300–1500 (cat. no. 101).

Opposite:
Plate 108. Human-Effigy Vessel, ceramic, Mississippian period, A.D. 1100–1300 (cat. no. 102).

Left:
Plate 109. Bowl with Head Adorno (Bell Plain), ceramic, Late Mississippian period, A.D. 1300–1500 (cat. no. 103).

Plate 110. Frog-Effigy Pipe, bauxite, Stirling phase, Cahokia culture, Late Mississippian period, A.D. 1000–1300 (cat. no. 104).

155

handle on one end and a hook on the other, which was used to
launch a spear. When several *atlatls* with all of their component
parts intact were recovered from Indian Knoll, a Late Archaic village site on the Green River in Kentucky, it was found that bannerstones fitted in the center of the *atlatl* between the handle and
the hook. Recent research suggests that bannerstones, tied to the
center of thin, willowy shafts, increased the spear-thrower's flexibility and contributed to a springy, whiplike action. Of all the various parts of the *atlatl*, the bannerstone exhibits by far the most
attention to careful manufacture and aesthetic effect.

Bannerstones from Indian Knoll were made of a variety of
visually attractive materials, including quartz, chalcedony, granite, and banded clay stone, all collected from disparate sources
and fastidiously ground and polished into immaculate prismoidal
or—more rarely—"butterfly" shapes **(pls. 1–6)**. Collections of
grave offerings from Indian Knoll burials frequently include bannerstones, often ceremonially "killed" or broken, sometimes, but
not always, with the complete *atlatl* (Moore 1916; W. S. Webb
1946). If nearly half of the burial instances of bannerstones at Indian Knoll did not appear with women or young children, one
might assume that *atlatls* accompanied the males of appropriate

Plate 112. Human-Effigy Pipe, bauxite, Stirling phase, Cahokia culture, Late Mississippian period, A.D. 1000–1300 (cat. no. 106).

age for hunting and warfare who used them. As with the marine-shell and copper ornaments which also served as burial offerings at Indian Knoll, bannerstones represented a symbolic value denoting status and social prestige.

Bannerstones made in a variety of ingenious forms from banded slate, speckled porphyry, and other exotic materials circulated throughout the Woodlands during the last three millenia B.C. **(pls. 1–12)**. Several varieties seem to have been produced regionally, suggesting small sub-cycles of exchange within the greater range of the artifact type. Occasionally, groups of bannerstones are found in caches, confirming their significance as valued items beyond any functional utility **(pl. 10)**. The wide range of materials and forms, often artfully combined, suggests that bannerstones circulated as valued exchange objects, as in the case of marine shell and copper. Thus they appear to have functioned primarily as primitive valuables, adopting the form—common to many Late Archaic valuables—of sumptuary implements.

The intensity of exchange activity throughout Woodlands history remains incomprehensible unless the motivation behind it is understood. The wealth represented by exotic trade materials and objects had value only to the extent that it could be converted

Overleaf:
Plate 113. *Birger Figurine,* bauxite, Stirling phase, Cahokia culture, Mississippian period, A.D. 1000–1250 (cat. no. 107).

Plate 114. *Keller Figurine,* bauxite, Stirling phase, Cahokia culture, Mississippian period, A.D. 1000–1250 (cat. no. 108).

159

into social recognition. The terminal point for all Woodlands trade cycles was the mortuary ritual, in which the primitive valuable became a burial offering used during an elaborate ceremony honoring the recent dead. We have seen that primitive valuables of the Late Archaic period used for burial offerings consisted primarily of ornaments and sumptuary implements made of exotic and precious trade materials. Objects of these kinds continued to appear in mortuary contexts through the Woodland and Mississippian periods. Representational objects reflecting a religious world view or the act of the funerary ritual itself only emerged as important forms of mortuary art during these later eras of Woodlands history.

Mortuary Art

As we have seen, rituals of the dead played a central social role throughout Woodlands history. In the context of the process of cyclical exchange, the mortuary ritual ''consumed'' valuables, removing them from the exchange networks and creating a demand for more (Winters 1968). Feasts, distributions of gifts, and the ex-

Plate 115. Long-Nosed-God Ear Ornaments, marine shell, Cahokia culture, Mississippian period, A.D. 1100–1200 (cat. no. 109.1–.3).

Plate 116. Repoussé Plaque Showing Dancing Figures, copper and pigment, Mississippian period, A.D. 1100–1300 (cat. no. 110).

160

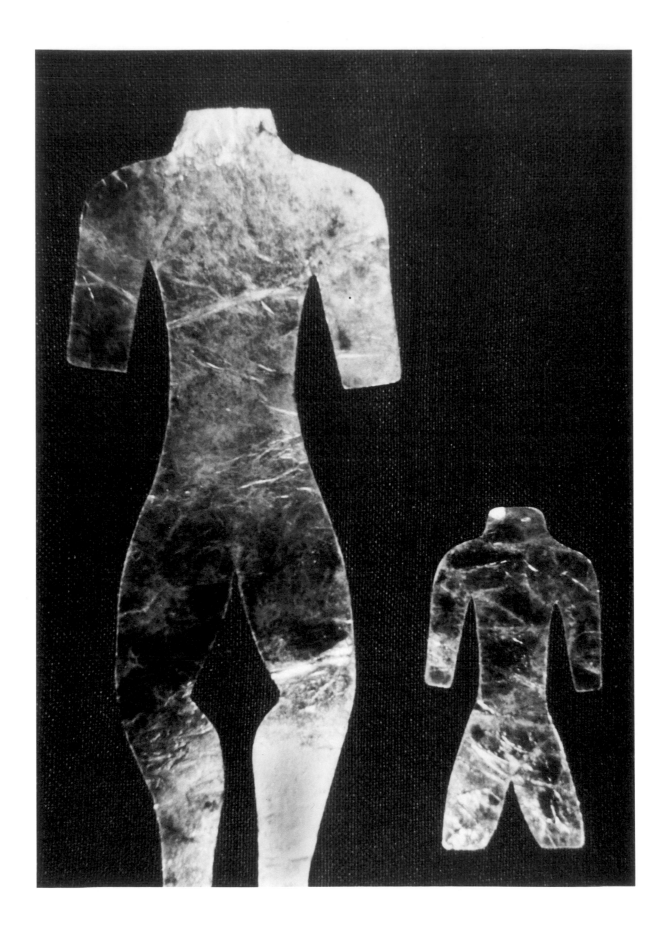

Opposite:
Figure 28. Effigies of headless human torsos, mica, l. 33.4 cm; l. 14 cm. Hopewell mound 25, Ross County, Ohio. Middle Woodland period, 200 B.C.–A.D. 400. Photo: Ohio Historical Society, Columbus.

Left:
Figure 29. *Wray Figurine*, stone. Newark, Licking County, Ohio. Middle Woodland period, 200 B.C.–A.D. 500. Photo: Ohio Historical Society, Columbus.

ercising of various kinds of ceremonial rights during the course of the mortuary ritual created and reaffirmed constellations of social relationships and obligations among individuals, families, and clans. Burial offerings attested to the social position of the deceased, and the gathering of materials for the offering focused the resources of the deceased's family, supporters, and sponsors. The mortuary ritual provided the occasion for the transformation of material wealth into social value. Although the deceased received goods representing considerable value, the living profited from this expenditure through enhanced status and high social regard.

Aside from the social event of the funeral, mortuary ritualism acted to confirm the transformation of an individual from living to dead. Death was not considered an absence of being, but rather a change of corporal state and a journey to another world where the deceased rejoined his ancestors. Funerary ritual assisted the deceased with this transition and insured that his spirit did not stay among the living where it might cause disease, bad luck, and other kinds of trouble (Underhill 1965:73–78). While some mortuary offerings simply equipped the dead for the journey and a new

Overleaf:
Plate 117. *Wulfing Plate* (Repoussé Plaque), copper, Mississippian period, A.D. 1200–1400 (cat. no. 111.1).

Plate 118. *Wulfing Plate* (Repoussé Plaque), copper, Mississippian period, AD. 1200–1400 (cat. no. 111.2).

Plate 119. *Wulfing Plate* (Repoussé Plaque), copper, Mississippian period, A.D. 1200–1400 (cat. no. 111.3).

Plate 120. *Wulfing Plate* (Repoussé Plaque), copper, Mississippian period, A.D. 1200–1400 (cat. no. 111.4).

state of being, others include cosmological references to the other-worldly destination of the deceased or refer, through their symbolism, to the process of ritualistic transformation from life to death, a process that engaged the entire social group.

Mortuary display and consumption of primitive valuables characterized many of the higher-status burials of the various Late Archaic traditions. As we have seen, large collections of marine shell; fastidiously made, but practically useless, flint blades; copper ornaments and tools; and stone pendants and gorgets of various kinds accompanied the favored dead. Since young to middle-aged men received a large proportion of these ostentatious offerings, it appears likely that successful entrepreneurs were often interred with their own wealth. Extravagant offerings to children and women suggest that family heads sponsored mortuary ceremonies for their kin or wards. It is possible that individuals expanded their influence among their social group by contributing to the funeral displays of others, thereby recruiting loyalty through the creation of reciprocal obligations. More importantly, funerary ritualism reinforced the structure of mutual interdependencies that characterized the larger kin group. Through this social forum the membership of the group was once again reaffirmed, embracing everyone from the achievement-oriented male or infirm elder to the helpless, dependent infant.

Since mortuary ritual helped to define the identity of the social group, be it family, clan, or band, it was important to schedule the ceremony so that the entire group could participate. Indian Knoll burials took place at a large campsite located along the banks of the Green River in Kentucky, where several family groups, separated all winter into small hunting territories, came together during the summer to gather plentiful and easily obtainable foods (Winters 1974). Bodies had to be preserved and cared for until such time as it became appropriate to perform the funeral ceremony. Their preservation prior to a final mortuary ritual became an important element in the ceremonial preparation of the dead, and a pattern of reburial or "bundle burial" became common during the Late Archaic period. As the dead accumulated between funerals, the ranks of mourners expanded, making the final ceremony relevant to more members of the group. If a funeral became more extravagant, more time might be necessary to gather together the resources for a significant ceremony. Meanwhile the dead had to be cared for until the ritual could be performed. One solution to this problem was the mortuary crypt or charnel house (fig. 14).

The Middle Woodland Havana people of the Illinois River divided themselves into small, fairly self-sufficient territories distributed along the river, each territory including portions of river

167

front, bottom lands, bluffs, and uplands. As we have seen, the territorial band established mortuary sites either on the bottom lands or, more frequently, on the bluffs overlooking the Illinois valley. As members of the band died, they were placed in the crypt with some initial ceremony in anticipation of a major mortuary ritual sometime in the future. The occasion of the final ritual appears to have been linked to the death of an important band member, who would be placed in the center of the crypt while the remains of others were scattered to the sides. At this point the crypt was buried beneath a mound of earth and a new crypt established.

Opposite:
Plate 121. Engraved Palette Stone, stone, Moundville culture, Mississippian period, A.D. 1200–1500 (cat. no. 112).

Left:
Plate 122. Engraved Palette Stone, stone, Moundville phase, Moundville culture, Mississippian period, A.D. 1200–1500 (cat. no. 113).

This procedure resulted in the development of mortuary mound groups in distinct bluff or bottom-land locations, each containing a large number of individuals associated with central log crypts. Throughout the period in which the crypt was in use, a wide range of materials, including Hopewell pottery (**pls. 57, 58**), platform pipes (**pls. 48–51**), ornaments, and so on, would be placed with the dead (Perino 1968).

The construction by the Ohio Hopewell of special charnel

Plate 123. Engraved Pendant, red slate, Moundville culture, Mississippian period, A.D. 1200–1500 (cat. no. 114).

houses, large wooden structures in which the dead were either cremated or buried in the floor, has already been described in detail. Preparing the body for burial seems to have been an important part of the funerary ritual. Several Hopewell art works illustrate aspects of this procedure. Copper and mica cutouts from Mound City and the Hopewell site depict headless, limbless torsos **(fig. 28)**. Some skeletal remains from Ohio Hopewell sites show deliberate disarticulation prior to burial, suggesting that the mortuary ritual included disassembling the body of the deceased. A unique stone sculpture from the Newark site in Ohio shows a man dressed in a bear costume with a detached head on his lap **(fig. 29)**. Here, very possibly, is an illustration of an episode of mortuary ritual in which a religious practitioner performs rites over the disarticulated remains of the deceased.

During the destruction of the charnel house and its burial beneath a large earth mound, large caches of trade materials and art

Plate 124. Beaker (Pensacola Engraved, var. Little Lagoon), ceramic (incising heightened with modern pigment), Mississippian period, A.D. 1200–1500 (cat. no. 115).

works sometimes were placed within the crematory altars or in other locations within the structure. Nearly all known art objects of the Ohio Hopewell come from burial mounds, where they played an important role in mortuary rituals **(pls. 34–47)**. Mortuary crypts and charnel houses functioned as family or clan mortuary centers, where the humblest members of the group could rely on their kinship affiliations to guarantee the proper treatment of their remains, no matter how peripherally located or poorly equipped, and where the group leaders received their just recognition (J. A. Brown 1979).

The kinship-oriented social structure of the Late Archaic and Woodland periods gave way to a more complex social system during the Mississippian period, when special status within the community stemmed from primogeniture within aristocratic lineages. Many Mississippian communities were ruled by chiefs who were

Plate 125. Engraved Jar (Walls Engraved), ceramic, Late Mississippian period, A.D. 1300–1600 (cat. no. 116).

Plate 126. Seated-Male-Effigy Pipe, banded slate, Mississippian period, A.D. 1100–1350 (cat. no. 117).

endowed with special religious powers and responsibilities. Some were considered to be the descendants of gods or powerful spirits. Their close relatives served as priests or war chiefs (Hudson 1976:202–234). These sacred individuals received special treatment during their funerary rites.

Most Mississippian individuals were buried in community cemeteries, while members of the highest-status lineages were placed in special mortuary temples at the time of their deaths. These mortuary temples are roughly related to the Middle Woodland concept of the charnel house. Hernando de Soto and other early visitors to the Southeast described temples on top of large platform mounds that contained the remains of the ancestors of the chief, kept in baskets and cared for by priests (Bourne 1904, I:101–102). Stone, terra cotta, or wooden images (pls. 96, 139–

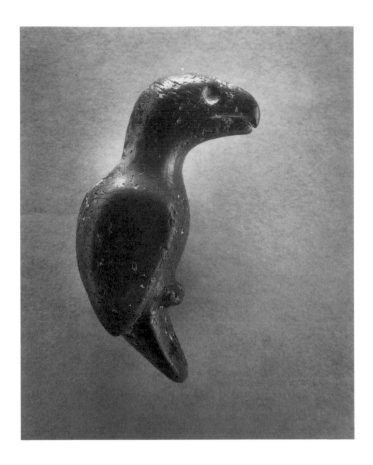

Plate 127. Bird-Effigy Pipe, stone, Early Mississippian period, A.D. 900–1300 (cat. no. 118).

141), possibly depicting the deceased or the founding ancestor or "culture hero" of the chiefly lineage, guarded the receptacles of bones (Moorehead 1932:11–14, 27–33; Swanton 1946:742–746; J. A. Brown 1975:13–17) (fig 14). After a long interval the accumulated remains of the dead were buried in the floor of the temple or around the circumference of the platform mound. Then, the temple was destroyed, the entire mound covered with a fresh mantle of earth, and a new temple erected on top.

During this episode of renewal, temple idols received burial treatment much like the honored deceased. The temple sculptures from the Etowah site were placed in mortuary crypts around the periphery of mound C (the mortuary temple platform) that were very much like those used for human remains (Moorehead 1932:11–14; Larson and Kelly 1957:43). The large Mississippian ancestor figures clearly participated in every phase of high-status mortuary ritualism (possibly as an evocation of the founding ancestor intended to supervise the proceedings or as a representation of the honored deceased as he had been in life), from the preparation and curation of the body in the mortuary temple to its ultimate placement within the mound itself.

Ritualistic processing of the honored dead in the mortuary

Plate 128. Crouching-Human-Effigy Pipe, sandstone, Little Egypt/Barnett phase, Lamar culture, Late Mississippian period, A.D. 1400–1600 (cat. no. 119).

temple apparently focused upon certain anatomical portions of the deceased, such as the head, hands, and the long bones of the legs. A large variety of art works depicts portions of human remains being treated in ritualistic ways. An engraved beaker from Moundville, for example, is decorated with a pattern of skulls and long bones (pl. 124). A common bottle form from the central Southeast includes appliqué representations of heads in varying states of dessication (fig. 30). Effigy-head vessels from various Mississippian locations, with slitlike eyes and grimacing mouths that replicate the expressions of death (pls. 91–93), probably depict honored remains preserved for ritual treatment. Several engraved shell designs from the Southeast illustrate ceremonially costumed individuals dancing or holding detached heads (figs. 12, 19). While it has been customary to describe these designs as warriors with trophy heads, studies of the remains of funeral ceremonies at major Mississippian sites have revealed that the separation of the body into differently treated parts was a frequent ritual procedure (J. A. Brown 1975:13–17).

Opposite:
Figure 30. Bottle, ceramic, h. 22.1 cm, diam. 20 cm. Dallas site, Hamilton County, Tennessee. Mississippian period, A.D. 1300–1500.

Left:
Plate 129. Seated-Human-Effigy Pipe, hematitic stone, Dallas phase, Dallas culture, Late Mississippian period, A.D. 1300–1500 (cat. no. 120).

Plate 130. Feline-Effigy Pipe, stone, Mississippian period, A.D. 1200–1500 (cat. no. 121).

The "hand-eye" motif, a hand design with an eye in the palm (pls. 121, 123), also fits into this category of imagery. Hands removed from the honored dead were sometimes buried separately, as in the case of a jar filled with hand remains recovered from the Great Mortuary in the Craig mound at the Spiro site (J. A. Brown 1975:15). The eye in the palm may symbolize the sun, since southeastern mythology describes the sun as a "blazing eye" (Swanton 1931:195). A cross sometimes was substituted for the eye in the palm (pl. 105). As we have seen, the cross within a circle was another important Mississippian sun symbol. Communities of the time identified their chiefs with the sun or believed them to be the sun's descendants, as in the case of the Natchez of the lower Mississippi valley (Swanton 1911:100–110). The hand-eye motif, then, depicts a select portion of the honored remains of a Mississippian chief, a "relic" containing great spiritual power.

Recognition of the dead through prescribed, carefully performed ceremonies reinforced the social relationships between individuals, families, and communities of the living throughout Woodlands history. The ritual provided a context for the display and consumption of ceremonial art works, and the form of the

179

ritual itself became a subject for artistic representation through the illustration of specific episodes or the use of visual symbols referring to treatment of the dead. The funerary ritual also confronted the living with the world outside their own experience: the realm of the afterlife and the universe beyond the terrestrial earth that the dead must rejoin. Many artistic objects and procedures associated with the funeral ceremony described this greater cosmos in an attempt to bridge the gap between the knowledge of the living and the experience of the dead.

World View and Cosmology

In many societies the underlying principles of world view and cosmological structure have been the most resistant to cultural change. Art—both the oral literature of myth and the plastic and graphic arts—creates a symbolic shorthand of metaphorical references that is used to describe the complexities and mysteries of a religious concept of the world during moments of social and personal ritual. Artistic continuities over several millenia of Native American history have stemmed not only from the preservation of traditional approaches to manufacturing and media, but, more importantly, from an ancient, underlying metaphorical construct of the universe that has dominated the iconography of Native American art history.

Throughout the Americas, traditional Native thought has conceived of the universe as a layered structure with the terrestrial domain suspended below the celestial vault of the sky-world and above the watery realm of the underworld. The horizontal axes of the earth have been defined by the four cardinal directions, whose conjunction has been thought of as creating the center—the world navel or world tree—connecting the earth with those above and below it. Passage from this world to the others can be accomplished only through a shaman's visionary journey or through death.

The sky and the underworld have been personified throughout North America by a pair of antithetical mythic beings: a celestial bird and an underwater monster. The celestial bird, often called the Thunderbird, has been envisioned as a gigantic, raptorial bird like an eagle, whose flapping wings create thunder and whose flashing eyes emit lightning. A monstrous, horned serpent—the piasa or Underwater Panther already mentioned—has been thought to rule over the underworld. These beings constantly engage in a life-and-death struggle. The earth, poised between the upper and underworlds, mediates between them. Man has acted to maintain a balance between these antithetical forces in

Plate 132. Dog-Effigy Vessel, ceramic, Late Mississippian period, A.D. 1300–1500 (cat. no. 123).

order to preserve health and well-being. On the other hand, the powers of the sky and the underworld have been used by man for healing, hunting and military success, or sorcery. Images of celestial birds and underwater monsters, serving as metaphorical references to the powers of the sky and the underworld, have functioned as symbols of special status or as ceremonial objects made to be manipulated during episodes of religious ritual. In all cases these images refer to religious mysteries and powers beyond man's everyday experience.

Analogues of the celestial bird include eagles, hawks, and falcons—in fact, nearly all avian creatures. Some of the earliest visual references to birds in Native American art can be seen on ground and polished birdstones, which appear to have functioned as *atlatl* appendages (**pls. 16–19**). They were coveted exchange items, sought after and traded throughout the Midwest and Great Lakes between 1500 and 500 B.C. (Townsend 1959). Birdstones stem from the tradition of the sumptuary implement as exemplified by bannerstones and elaborate copper and flint blades, but with the added cosmological significance of references to birds and the powers of the sky.

Bird imagery also played a significant iconographic role at Poverty Point, the important Late Archaic site in the lower Mississippi valley. As we have seen, the major monument marking the site, an earthen mound nearly seventy feet tall, 710 feet wide, and 640 feet long, is shaped like a bird, oriented westward with wings extended, thereby paralleling the daily route of the sun (**fig. 2**). Small ground beads made of polished red jasper found at this site were carved in the form of birds. Birds with outstretched wings also appear on a relief-carved steatite bowl and an incised red jasper plummet (**pl. 28**) found there (C. H. Webb 1968, 1977; Gibson 1983). Beads from Poverty Point were carved in the shape of owls (**pl. 24**), whose nighttime habits, according to Creek and Cherokee thinking, associated them with the activities of sorcerers and witches (Hudson 1976:130). Owls become an important image during the subsequent Woodland period, appearing on Weeden Island ceramics from Florida and Hopewell-related effigy platform pipes from Ohio and Illinois. The emphasis on bird forms at Poverty Point anticipated an important focus of Woodlands iconography for several centuries thereafter.

Some of the elaborate compositions visible on Hopewell pottery from Ohio, Illinois, and Louisiana contain bird designs executed in a complex, zoned style. This style dates from the first two hundred years A.D. Often the designs include pairs of birds opposed in bilateral symmetry or repeated single birds with scrolls and spirals indicating wings, tails, and talons (**pls. 57, 58**). This

Plate 133. Engraved Shell Gorget Showing Two Bird-Men, marine shell, Dallas phase, Dallas culture, Late Mississippian period, A.D. 1300–1500 (cat. no. 124).

imagery and its stylistic interpretation were widely dispersed due to the expansion of Middle Woodland exchange networks, suggesting that trade relationships between far-flung regional traditions engendered ideological exchange and stylistic diffusion beyond the simple transfer of special trade materials.

Two kinds of bird images appeared at this time: a raptorial bird with a curving, rapacious beak and a broad-billed duck. All three Hopewell pottery traditions—the Havana of Illinois, Marksville of Louisiana, and Ohio Hopewell—made pots with both designs (figs. 6, 31; pls. 57, 58). The designs, which often appear together at the same site or within the same burial mound, clearly complement each other, the raptor evoking an association with the sky, the duck referring to the watery underworld. Ducks and raptorial birds comprise the only representational imagery on Hopewell pottery, although other designs may also be cosmological referents. While ducks and raptorial birds never appear together on the same pot, the two designs describe a cohesive universe structure.

Bird designs similar to those of the Hopewell appear on engraved Adena tablets, a unique group of carved, tabular stones that apparently were used to reproduce such designs on other materials. The bilateral symmetry of the *Wilmington Tablet* design (pl. 31) and the extended profile bird form of the *Berlin Tablet* (pl. 32) closely parallel the stylistic conventions visible on Hopewell pottery. No duck images appear, but several of the engraved Adena tablets include designs suggesting horned monsters. The corpus of these tablets and stylistically related Hopewell pottery is evidence of an emerging iconographic system in which the opposed forces of the layered cosmos were expressed metaphorically via stylistically consistent images of specific mythic creatures.

The celestial bird and horned monster found a wide range of expression in the art of the Ohio Hopewell, in objects of mica and copper and in other sculpted materials. At least three burials at the Hopewell site were equipped with images of flying eagles cut from beaten copper (Moorehead 1922:265) (fig. 25; pl. 37). Similar copper falcon images came from an important mortuary ritual location at Mound City (Mills 1922:490) (pl. 38). A pair of bird talons, cut in silhouette from mica (pl. 35), accompanied a buried couple at the Hopewell site, along with a graceful mica hand (Shetrone 1926:95) (pl. 34). Stone objects of various kinds placed with the dead at Ohio Hopewell mortuary sites often were sculpted in the forms of birds, primarily raptors (pls. 41, 42, 44).

Other Ohio Hopewell objects placed in important ritual locations depict various forms of horned underwater monsters. A crematory altar in mound 4 of the Turner site in Hamilton County, Ohio, contained several sculpted representations of horned monsters (Willoughby and Hooton 1922:63). A carved boatstone represents a gruesome, monstrous creature with a fat serpent's body, four bovine-like horns, short, stubby legs, and a rattlesnake's tail (pl. 43). A second boatstone was engraved with a fantastic aquatic animal having a bottle-like snout and spiral tail. These two objects flanked a group of naturalistically modeled human figurines made of terra cotta, and the entire ensemble was overlaid by a large, twisted, horned serpent cut from sheet mica.

All of the representations of monstrous beings are consistent with historic-period representations of underworld spirits such as the Horned Serpent and Underwater Panther. The assembled objects may be interpreted as an evocation of the burial group en route to the Land of the Dead, with the cremated deceased represented by the group of figurines and the underworld journey implied by the host of underworld creatures. Many historic-period Native groups believed that the road of the dead passed through the underworld, which was inhabited by a variety of monstrous creatures who had to be avoided or overcome (Barnouw 1977:136).

Another large serpent head (fig. 32) and a pair of fish, all

Figure 32. Serpent-head effigy, copper. Hopewell mound 25, Ross County, Ohio. Middle Woodland period, 200 B.C.–A.D. 400. Photo: Field Museum of Natural History, Chicago.

185

Plate 134. Engraved Gorget
Showing a Winged Figure,
marine shell, Wibanks phase,
Etowah culture, Mississippian
period, A.D. 1200–1450 (cat.
no. 125).

Plate 135. Engraved Shell
Gorget Showing a Spider
Motif, marine shell, Dallas
phase, Dallas culture, Late
Mississippian period, A.D.
1300–1500 (cat. no. 126).

made of sheet copper, were placed amid a large cache of copper
objects in mound 25, the largest and most important mortuary
structure at the Hopewell site. Fish, as underwater creatures, have
served as analogues for the underworld in historic Native thought.
Several individuals in this mound wore antlered headdresses
made of copper; similar headdresses with antlers and horns were
found at crematory locations at Mound City. One might assume
that antlers would logically be associated with deer, but more often antlers and horns have symbolized horned serpents in historic
Native contexts. The priests of the Wyandot fish clan, for example,
wore deer antlers on their heads and called themselves ''snake-
men'' (Barbeau 1952:117).

Visual references to underwater monsters and celestial birds
increased dramatically during the Mississippian period. These

mythic creatures maintained their cosmological associations, but were grafted and adapted to new concepts: cults of agricultural fertility, of warrior societies, and of chiefly ancestors. The spiritual importance of the upper world increased dramatically, since the celestial portion of the cosmos possessed the warming, light-producing sun, which became of paramount importance to Mississippian religion. As we have seen, the Natchez, a Mississippian people that survived culturally until their eighteenth-century wars with the French, called their chief the "Great Sun"; he was believed to be the sun's descendant.

A sacred fire, symbolizing the powers of the sun, burned perpetually in the major Natchez temple, cared for by priests who were generally the Great Sun's close relatives. The fire was fed by four logs arranged like a cross and oriented to the four cardinal directions (Swanton 1911:100–110; Hudson 1976:132), recalling the cross-in-circle symbol already mentioned. Fire was thought to have come to earth originally as a lightning bolt sent by Thunderbirds that ignited a sycamore tree on an island. A water spider succeeded in retrieving fire from the island, after many other animals had failed, by carrying coals upon its back across the water (Mooney 1900:239–240). The water spider, sometimes with a circle and cross on its back, may also be considered a sun symbol as the bringer of the sacred fire (pl. 135).

The most common bird image of the Mississippian period is the peregrine falcon, which became an important symbol of military prowess because of its speed and aggressiveness. As we have seen, in Mississippian art the falcon is often combined with a human figure, implying a falcon impersonator or costumed dancer. Spirit beings in Native religion may transform themselves from animal to human shape at will, so that mixtures of human and falcon anatomy in Mississippian art probably were intended to stress the powerful, spiritual character of the falcon. The set of eight *Wulfing Plates*, cut copper repoussé objects found in a cache just outside St. Louis (pls. 117–120), illustrates a sequence of falcon-man transformations. Similiar falcon-men, or falcon spirits, who may have acted as spirit guardians of high-status Mississippian warriors, appear on shell and copper objects throughout the Southeast (figs. 12, 19–21; pls. 133, 134).

The "weeping-eye mask," a type of marine-shell mask found throughout much of the Woodlands region during the late Mississippian period, consists of a face having falcon-eye markings with the addition of thunderbolt zigzags descending from the eyes. These suggest that the falcon, in this context, has been merged with the lightning-producing Thunderbird concept (pl. 137).

Horned serpents also continued to be important elements of iconography during the Mississippian period. Pairs of horned ser-

Plate 137. Engraved Weeping-Eye Mask, marine shell, Barnett phase, Lamar culture, Late Mississippian period, A.D. 1500–1600 (cat. no. 128).

Plate 138. Spaghetti-Style Engraved Shell Gorget, marine shell, Dallas phase, Dallas culture, Late Mississippian period, A.D. 1300–1500 (cat. no. 129).

Plate 139. Seated Male Figurine, sandstone, Late Mississippian period, A.D. 1300–1500 (cat. no. 130).

pents appear on a series of engraved paint palettes from Moundville in Alabama. These large stone disks were used to grind pigments and medicines for rituals. While simple, undecorated examples come from several southeastern sites, the elaborate engraved ones are concentrated at Moundville. Their iconographic treatment suggests that they were important ritual objects reserved for the local elite. One palette-stone design shows a pair of horned serpents tied together, encircling a hand-eye motif (pl. 121). As we have seen, the hand-eye motif was linked to high-status Mississippian mortuary rituals. The encircling serpents with their underworld associations reinforce the theme of death by evoking the journey of the dead.

While horned serpents and celestial birds appear in a variety of Mississippian contexts, their attributes are often combined, as in the case of a winged serpent or horned rattlesnake with wings, which appears on Mississippian pottery (pl. 125) and engraved marine-shell containers. The mixture of bird and serpent attributes seems to have been an attempt to harmonize antithetical powers in a unified, reconciliatory symbol of greater potency than images of one or the other.

A great deal of southeastern ritual was directed toward the restoration or maintenance of a balance between disjunctive forces. Disease, for example, was thought to result from spiritual pollution, which disrupted a natural balance and could be cured by the application of a substance or power considered to be the opposite of the polluting substance or power (Hudson 1976:336–351). The winged serpent, therefore, can be considered as a symbol of cosmological unity, since it brings together attributes of the sky and underworld. An engraved shell design from the Craig mound at Spiro (pl. 102) shows a group of four winged serpents surrounding a circle and cross motif, which is simultaneously a sun symbol—due to its reference to the sacred fire—and, as we have seen, a symbol of the four cardinal directions. Through its arrangement of cosmological symbols, this composition describes the horizontal and vertical axes of the universe and becomes a cosmological diagram.

The preponderance of bird and serpent imagery over more than two thousand years of Woodlands art history confirms the notion that a system of metaphorical references composed of these symbols became fixed in Native American cosmological thinking and artistic conventions at a very early date. As the social emphases of art changed, the images adopted new meanings and contexts, but still maintained their direct associations with basic Native American assumptions regarding the composition of the universe. Throughout their history, the images remained potent

Plate 140. Seated Male Figurine, sandstone, Wibanks phase, Etowah culture, Mississippian period, A.D. 1200–1450 (cat. no. 131).

as symbols of social influence and power as well as appearing in the iconography of the dead.

Although celestial birds and underwater monsters represented the primary powers of the universe, Woodlands Indians recognized a host of other spiritual identities that took part in more personal aspects of Native religion. Animals of all kinds often were considered to be spirit emissaries from other worlds who were willing to bestow gifts of power on those who sought them out. While celestial birds and underwater monsters symbolized the ultimate mysteries of Native religion, then, most direct contact with spiritual powers among Native people came through interactions with animal spirits, either through dreams or spirit quests.

Images of animals predominate in Woodlands art throughout all phases of its history. Some of the earliest representational art works from the region depict animals in various forms. A sandal-sole gorget, made of marine shell and dating to the Late Archaic period, contains an engraved rendering of a bear or opossum with an extended umbilical cord that encircles the body (pl. 21). Depictions of powerful animal spirits in historic-period Native art often emit "power lines" from different important body locations: the head, the mouth, or the navel.

While animals may appear on early ornaments and other kinds of ceremonial objects from the Woodlands, a wide range of naturalistic depictions occurs most frequently on Early and Middle Woodland smoking pipes. Pipe ritualism, central to any Native North American religious ceremony of the historic period, emerges in the archaeological record during the Late Archaic era. Smoking a pipe constituted an offering to the spirit world and functioned almost like a prayer, a request to spirit powers to attend and witness a religious or social event. The earliest pipes were simple stone or fired-clay tubes. Tubular pipes carved into animal or (rarely) human forms were made by the Early Woodland Adena (fig. 5; pl. 33). By the beginning of the Middle Woodland period, an impressive sculptural tradition of pipe carving had been established in several regions.

The smoking pipe and the image of an animal were combined in Native American art most likely because the animal spirit was the religious focus of the individual just as pipe smoking was an individual religious act. The kinds of animals that appear on Middle Woodland effigy pipes are those who often acted as spirit guardians or spirit protectors of individuals. The oral record of historic Woodlands peoples is rich in accounts of spiritual encounters between men seeking power and animals who granted gifts of medicines for healing, hunting, or warfare.

Many of the Middle Woodland effigy pipes depict birds—wrens, ravens, falcons, cardinals, and so on—who possessed powers drawn from the upper world (pls. 47, 50, 51). Animals associated with the underworld, such as snakes, turtles, frogs, otters, beavers, and bears (who live under the ground during winter) also appear (pls. 48, 49), as well as coyotes, bobcats, raccoons, cougars, and many other species (pl. 46). Nearly all of these effigy pipes evidence a strictly naturalistic approach to their animal subjects, reproducing textures of fur, patterns of feathers, species-specific markings, and even characteristic "gestures" and postures. It is clear that the pipe images represent terrestrial animals, not cosmological deities, although these animals were nevertheless endowed with the ability to offer spiritual powers.

The effigy platform pipe tradition of the Ohio Hopewell was concentrated at the Tremper and Mound City sites, where large caches numbering well over a hundred pipes were placed in crematory altars (pls. 46, 47). These probably belonged to many of the individuals who were cremated and interred at the sites and deposited there with the caches over an extended period of time. Several of these pipes show signs of long use and indigenous repair.

Individual pipes accompanied status burials within the Crab Orchard and Havana traditions of Illinois (pls. 48–51). Stylistically, these pipes resemble those from Ohio, suggesting that Illinois platform pipes were traded from the Ohio centers. Illinois pipes, however, are made of distinctive materials and display subtle peculiarities of style that make this assumption doubtful, although clearly there was a close artistic relationship between these two pipe-making traditions. Effigy platform pipes appear more sporadically in the Southeast, and most of them were also made locally.

After the first century A.D., a large number of steatite pipes, larger in size and less detailed in execution, began to circulate throughout the greater Woodlands region. Although these pipes are called Copena "great pipes" because they seem to have come from the Middle Woodland Copena complex located in the Tennessee valley close to several sources of steatite, only one has ever actually been found at a Copena site (fig. 33). Several were recovered from the Ohio Hopewell Seip site, one from the Mann site (pl. 61) in southern Indiana, and even one from the upper Illinois River; most finds have clustered among the middle southern states near the Appalachians. Copena pipes retain the emphasis on animals seen in the slightly earlier platform pipe tradition, although now the effigy consists of the tubular platform of the pipe rather than of the bowl (pls. 60, 62, 63).

A steatite pipe-making tradition apparently endured through the Mississippian period. Mississippian ritual pipes are larger and iconographically more ambitious. Many include human figures:

Overleaf:
Plate 141. Seated Female and Male Figurines, marble, Wibanks phase, Etowah culture, Mississippian period, A.D. 1200–1450 (cat. no. 132.1–.2).

Figure 33. Dog-effigy pipe, steatite. Copena mound, Alabama. Middle Woodland period, A.D. 200–600.

males involved in warfare either as costumed warriors or as bound prisoners **(pls. 98, 112, 131)**, or females in tableaux with agricultural themes **(pls. 113, 114)**. Animal imagery paralleling that of Middle-Woodland-period pipes was now shifted to ceramics. Effigy vessels depicting a wide range of species such as bears **(pl. 88)**, turtles **(pls. 84, 89)**, frogs **(pl. 87)**, and birds **(pl. 86)** accompany Mississippian cemetery burials. In fact, pottery was the most common Mississippian burial offering in a mortuary system in which more people received some things, but fewer people received the highest-status objects. As had been the case earlier, animal imagery reflected a more general and individualized level of religious practice than the cosmological imagery reserved for the social elite.

It is fair to assume that Native North American religious practices and beliefs underwent a great deal of change during some three thousand years of history. However, the raw materials of religious thought, the basic world view—or at least the system of visual metaphors used to describe the cosmos—remained surprisingly consistent over this same period of time. Indeed, the dichotomy between celestial bird and underwater monster and the spiritual significance of animals remain constant in traditional Native American religious thinking of the present day.

CHECKLIST

Editor's Note: References listed in most of the entries have been divided into two groups. Those following the initial colon include discussions or illustrations of the specific work(s) under consideration. Those following "See" include general discussions of similar or related objects, their functions, decoration, styles, etc., and the contexts in which they were made. The plate number at the end of each entry refers to the illustration in this book. In ceramics entries the ware-type names in parentheses (for example, "Havana Zoned") are documented by appropriate references to type descriptions.

1.1
Bannerstone
Chalcedony; h. 6.2 cm, w. 8.9 cm
Indian Knoll, Ohio County, Kentucky
Indian Knoll culture, Late Archaic
  period, 3000–2000 B.C.
The Museum of the American Indi-
  an, Heye Foundation, New York
  17/409
References: Moore 1916: pl. 12. See
  also W. S. Webb 1946:267–270,
  319ff.
Plate 1

1.2
Bannerstone
Granite; h. 7.5 cm, w. 5.7 cm
Indian Knoll, Ohio County, Kentucky
Indian Knoll culture, Late Archaic
  period, 3000–2000 B.C.
The Museum of the American Indi-
  an, Heye Foundation, New York
  17/1925
References: Moore 1916:466, pl.
  10d. See also W. S. Webb 1946:
  267–270, 319ff.
Plate 2

1.3
Bannerstone
Chalcedony; h. 6 cm, w. 5.5 cm
Indian Knoll, Ohio County, Kentucky
Indian Knoll culture, Late Archaic
  period, 3000–2000 B.C.
The Museum of the American Indi-

an, Heye Foundation, New York
  17/1928
References: Moore 1916:467, pl. 10c.
  See also W. S. Webb 1946:267–
  270, 319ff.
Plate 3

1.4
Bannerstone
Siliceous rock; h. 7.7 cm, w. 6.2 cm
Indian Knoll, Ohio County, Kentucky
Indian Knoll culture, Late Archaic
  period, 3000–2000 B.C.
The Museum of the American Indi-
  an, Heye Foundation, New York
  17/1929
References: Moore 1916:462, pl. 10i.
  See also W. S. Webb 1946:267–
  270, 319ff.
Plate 4

1.5
Bannerstone
  Banded clay stone; h. 6.9 cm, w.
  5 cm
Indian Knoll, Ohio County, Kentucky
Indian Knoll culture, Late Archaic
  period, 3000–2000 B.C.
The Museum of the American Indi-
  an, Heye Foundation, New York
  17/1930
References: Moore 1916:464, pl. 11f.
  See also W. S. Webb 1946:267–
  270, 319ff.
Plate 5

1.6
Bannerstone
Banded clay stone; h. 6.9 cm, w. 5.6 cm
Ohio County, Kentucky
Indian Knoll culture, Late Archaic period, 3000–2000 B.C.
The Museum of the American Indian, Heye Foundation, New York 20/3181
Reference: See W. S. Webb 1946: 267–270, 319ff.
Plate 6

2
Bannerstone
Banded slate; h. 9.7 cm, w. 5 cm
Wells County, Indiana
Late Archaic period, 2000–1000 B.C.
Found by William Baley, 1854
The Gordon Hart Collection, Bluffton, Indiana
References: Moorehead 1910, I:396 (ill.); 1917:115
Plate 7

3
Notched Ovate Bannerstone
Banded slate; h. 12.7 cm, w. 14 cm
Michigan
Late Archaic period, 2000–1000 B.C.
The Gordon Hart Collection, Bluffton, Indiana
Plate 8

4
Butterfly-Shaped Bannerstone
Banded slate; h. 11.4 cm, w. 12.7 cm
Seneca County, Ohio
Late Archaic period, 3000–1000 B.C.
The Gordon Hart Collection, Bluffton, Indiana
Plate 9

5
Knobbed Lunate Bannerstone
Banded slate; h. 12 cm, w. 17.7 cm
Mound near Wood River, Madison County, Illinois
Late Archaic/Early Woodland period, 1000–500 B.C.
Ex-coll. Paul Titterington
The Gordon Hart Collection, Bluffton, Indiana
Reference: Knoblock 1939:33–34, pl. 4
Plate 10

6
Oval Bannerstone
Sandstone; h. 10.6 cm, w. 12.5 cm
Sequatchie County, Tennessee
Lauderdale culture, Late Archaic period, 2000–1000 B.C.
Thomas Gilcrease Institute of American History and Art, Tulsa, Oklahoma 6123.909
Plate 11

7
Bannerstone
Porphyry; h. 7.1 cm, w. 9.1 cm
Hemplull site, Brown County, Illinois
Titterington complex, Late Archaic period, 1500–500 B.C.
Thomas Gilcrease Institute of American History and Art, Tulsa, Oklahoma 6123.1211
References: Knoblock 1939:203–204, pl. 98, no. 1. See also Snyder 1962:230–274
Plate 12

8.1
Socketed Blade
Copper; l. 59.5 cm, w. 7.5 cm
Burial on ridge overlooking Lake Superior, Houghton County, Michigan
Old Copper complex, Late Archaic period, 1500–500 B.C.
Excavated by Isaac Ottis, during construction of Portage Lake–Lake Superior ship canal, 1872
The National Museum of Natural History, Smithsonian Institution, Washington, D.C. 204154
Plate 13

8.2
Knife
Copper; l. 38.5 cm, w. 4.5 cm
Burial on ridge overlooking Lake Superior, Houghton County, Michigan
Old Copper complex, Late Archaic period, 1500–500 B.C.
Excavated by Isaac Ottis, during construction of Portage Lake–Lake Superior ship canal, 1872
The National Museum of Natural History, Smithsonian Institution, Washington, D.C. 204156
Plate 14

9.1–.2
Serrated Tanged Blade; Crescent Knife

Copper; 1. 12.2 cm; 1. 15.8 cm

Maple Creek, Outagamie County, Wisconsin; Dale, Outagamie County, Wisconsin

Old Copper complex, Late Archaic period, 2000–1000 B.C.

Ex-coll. Frederick S. Perkins; sold to Smithsonian Institution, 1890

The National Museum of Natural History, Smithsonian Institution, Washington, D.C. 147580; 147293

Plate 15

10.1–.3
Three Birdstones

Granitic porphyry; slate (limonite stain); green Huronian slate; h. 3.7 cm, 1. 8.2 cm; h. 3.9 cm, 1. 12.5 cm; h. 3.3 cm, 1 8.8 cm

Andrews site, Bay County, Michigan

Red Ocher complex, Late Archaic period, 1500–1000 B.C.

University of Michigan Museum of Anthropology, Ann Arbor 40176; 40191; 40254

References: Townsend 1959:219, 224, pl. 67a; Fitting 1975:84–85, fig. 31

Plate 16

11
Popeyed Birdstone

Speckled porphyry; h. 5 cm, l. 8.5 cm

Berrien County, Michigan

Red Ocher/Glacial Kame complex, Late Archaic/Early Woodland period, 1500–500 B.C.

The Robin B. Martin Collection

Plate 17

12
Popeyed Birdstone

Porphyry; h. 5.9 cm, l. 11.5 cm

Michigan

Red Ocher/Glacial Kame complex, Late Archaic/Early Woodland period, 1500–1000 B.C.

Thomas Gilcrease Institute of American History and Art, Tulsa, Oklahoma 6123.1153

Plate 18

13
Popeyed Birdstone

Banded slate; w. 3.6 cm, l. 10 cm

Washtenaw County, Michigan

Red Ocher/Glacial Kame complex,

Late Archaic/Early Woodland period, 1500–500 B.C.

Found by Mrs. Dorothy Cook of Ypsilanti, Michigan, 1983

The Detroit Institute of Arts 1983.322

Plate 19

14
Gorget

Cannel coal; l. 20.4 cm

Allen County, Indiana

Glacial Kame complex, Late Archaic/Early Woodland period, 1500–500 B.C.

Ex-coll. Leslie Hill, Fort Wayne, Indiana, 1901; ex-coll. Dr. Roland Bunch, Muncie, Indiana, 1928; ex-coll. Charles Smith, Modoc, Indiana, 1949

The Gordon Hart Collection, Bluffton, Indiana

Reference: *Central States Archaeological Journal* 1960:29, fig. 13

Plate 20

15
Sandal-Sole Gorget

Marine shell; l. 19.4 cm, w. 7.2 cm

Hardin County, Ohio

Glacial Kame complex, Late Archaic/Early Woodland period, 1500–500 B.C.

Ohio Historical Society, Columbus 190/3

Reference: Cunningham 1948: pl. 6, fig. 2

Plate 21

16.1–.2
Two Rectangular Gorgets

Quartz; 1. 15.5 cm, w. 7.1 cm; l. 14.4 cm, w. 7.9 cm

Hemplull site, Brown County, Illinois

Early Woodland period, 1000–500 B.C.

Thomas Gilcrease Institute of American History and Art, Tulsa, Oklahoma 6123.1208; 6123.1210

References: Knoblock 1939:203–204, pl. 98, no. 7. See also Snyder 1962:230–274

Plate 22

17
Locust-Shaped Bead
Red jasper; h. 3 cm, l. 5.7 cm
Badlow Creek, near Mars Hill, La-
fayette County, Arkansas
Poverty Point culture, Late Archaic
period, 1500–700 B.C.
Found by Oscar Lee on property of J.
T. Lee, 1885
Thomas Gilcrease Institute of Ameri-
can History and Art, Tulsa, Okla-
homa 6123.2964
Reference: see C. H. Webb 1971
Plate 23

18.1–.2
Two Owl-Effigy Beads
Jasper; h. 2.8 cm, w. 1.6 cm; h. 1.1
cm, w. 0.8 cm
Poverty Point site [16WC5], West
Carroll Parish, Louisiana
Poverty Point culture, Late Archaic
period, 1500–700 B.C.
The Alexander Collection, Epps,
Louisiana
References: C. H. Webb 1977:61,
figs. 19, 21. See also Ford and
Webb 1956
Plate 24

19
Animal-Effigy Bead
Jasper; h. 0.9 cm, l. 1.1 cm
Lower Jackson site [16WC10], West
Carroll Parish, Louisiana
Poverty Point culture, Late Archaic
period, 1500–700 B.C.
The Dennis Labatt Collection, Epps,
Louisiana
Plate 25

20
Clamshell-Effigy Bead
Jasper; h. 1.6 cm, w. 1.4 cm
Poverty Point site [16WC5], West
Carroll Parish, Louisiana
Poverty Point culture, Late Archaic
period, 1500–700 B.C.
The Alexander Collection, Epps,
Louisiana
References: C. H. Webb 1968:316,
figs. 7x, x′; idem. 1977:61, fig. 39.
See also Ford and Webb 1956
Plate 26

21
Blade-Shaped Pendant
Red jasper; h. 7.9 cm, w. 4.6 cm

Bayou Maçon, West Carroll Parish,
Louisiana
Poverty Point culture, Late Archaic
period, 1500–700 B.C.
Thomas Gilcrease Institute of Ameri-
can History and Art, Tulsa, Okla-
homa 6123.2962
Reference: C. H. Webb 1977:61, fig.
55
Plate 27

22
Engraved Plummet Showing a Bird
Red jasper; h. 8.65 cm, diam. 2.9 cm
Floyd area, Bayou Maçon, West Car-
roll Parish, Louisiana
Poverty Point culture, Late Archaic
period, 1500–700 B.C.
Thomas Gilcrease Institute of Ameri-
can History and Art, Tulsa, Okla-
homa 6123.2596
Plate 28

23
Plummet
Hematite; h. 8.6 cm, diam. 2.6 cm
Bayou Maçon, West Carroll Parish,
Louisiana
Poverty Point culture, Late Archaic
period, 1500–700 B.C.
Thomas Gilcrease Institute of Ameri-
can History and Art, Tulsa, Okla-
homa 6123.2658
Plate 29

24
Human Figurine
Terra cotta; h. 4.8 cm, w. 2.65 cm
Poverty Point site, West Carroll Par-
ish, Louisiana
Poverty Point culture, Late Archaic
period, 1500–700 B.C.
Thomas Gilcrease Institute of Ameri-
can History and Art, Tulsa, Okla-
homa 6123.5424.5739
Reference: See C. H. Webb 1968:310
Plate 30

25
Wilmington Tablet
Sandstone; h. 9.8 cm, w. 12.8
Clinton County, Ohio
Late Adena culture, Middle Wood-
land period, 400 B.C.–A.D. 1
Ohio Historical Society, Columbus
3490/210
References: Welch and Richardson
1881:40–48, fig. 1; Greenman

1932:512 (ill.); Webb and Haag 1940:6–134 (esp. 121), fig. 65; Webb and Baby 1957:86, fig. 34; Otto 1975:31–36; Penney 1980:3–38, fig. 3

Plate 31

26
Berlin Tablet
Sandstone; h. 7.1 cm, w. 14.3 cm
Jackson County, Ohio
Late Adena culture, Middle Woodland period, 400 B.C.–A.D. 1
Ohio Historical Society, Columbus
References: Sylvester 1879:73–75, 72 (ill.); Webb and Haag 1940:6–134 (esp. 120), fig. 64; Webb and Baby 1957:85, fig. 33; Otto 1975:31–36; Penney 1980:3–38, fig. 9

Plate 32

27
Modified Platform Effigy Pipe
Stone; h. 6.1 cm, l. 18.6 cm
Mound in Neward area, Licking County, Ohio
Late Adena culture, Middle Woodland period, 400 B.C.–A.D. 1
Ex-coll. William Clogston
Peabody Museum of Archaeology and Ethnology, Harvard University, Cambridge, Massachusetts 78-52-10/15667

Plate 33

28
Hand-Shaped Cutout
Sheet mica; h. 29 cm, w. 16 cm
Mound 25, Hopewell site, Ross County, Ohio
Ohio Hopewell culture, Middle Woodland period, 200 B.C.–A.D. 400
Ohio Historical Society, Columbus 283/294
Reference: Shetrone 1926: fig. 143

Plate 34

29
Bird-Claw-Shaped Cutout
Sheet mica; l. 28 cm, w. 17 cm
Mound 25, Hopewell site, Ross County, Ohio
Ohio Hopewell culture, Middle Woodland period, 200 B.C.–A.D. 400
Ohio Historical Society, Columbus 283/292–2
Reference: Shetrone 1926: fig. 143

Plate 35

30
Human Profile Cutout
Sheet mica; h. 17.5 cm, w. 13.1 cm
Mound 3, Turner site, Hamilton County, Ohio
Ohio Hopewell culture, Middle Woodland period, A.D. 200–400
Peabody Museum of Archaeology and Ethnology, Harvard University, Cambridge, Massachusetts 82-35-10/30002
Reference: Willoughby and Hooton 1922:56, pl. 15

Plate 36

31
Eagle-Shaped Cutout
Copper; h. 9 cm, l. 21.9 cm
Hopewell site, Ross County, Ohio
Ohio Hopewell culture, Middle Woodland period, 200 B.C.–A.D. 400
Excavated by Warren K. Moorehead, 1891; ex-coll. Paul Titterington; ex-coll. E. K. Pettrie, Brown Lake, Wisconsin
The Gordon Hart Collection, Bluffton, Indiana

Plate 37

32
Falcon-Shaped Cutout
Copper; h. 20.4 cm, l. 30.6 cm
Mound 7, Mound City, Ross County, Ohio
Ohio Hopewell culture, Middle Woodland period, 200 B.C.–A.D. 1
The Mound City Group National Monument, National Parks Service, Chillicothe, Ohio 28/27
Reference: Mills 1922:489–491, fig. 60

Plate 38

33
Cutout Plaque
Copper; h. 13.4 cm, l. 24.2 cm
Mound 7, Mound City, Ross County, Ohio
Ohio Hopewell culture, Middle Woodland period, 200 B.C.–A.D. 1
The Mound City Group National Monument, National Parks Service, Chillicothe, Ohio 28/28
Reference: Mills 1922:489–491, fig. 63

Plate 39

34
Repoussé Plaque Showing Four Birds
Copper; h. 14 cm, w. 25.5 cm
Mound 7, Mound City, Ross County, Ohio
Ohio Hopewell culture, Middle Woodland period, 200 B.C.–A.D. 1
The Mound City Group National Monument, National Parks Service, Chillicothe, Ohio 28/29
Reference: Mills 1922:489–491, fig. 62
Plate 40

35
Eagle-Effigy Boatstone
Pipestone, river pearl; h. 3.3 cm, l. 9.2 cm
Mound 25, Hopewell site, Ross County, Ohio
Ohio Hopewell culture, Middle Woodland period, 200 B.C.–A.D. 400
Ohio Historical Society, Columbus 283/113
Reference: Moorehead 1922:73–181 (esp. 112), pl. 83, no. 2
Plate 41

36
Duck-Effigy Boatstone
Stone; h. 2.7 cm, l. 9 cm
Seip mound, Ross County, Ohio
Ohio Hopewell, Middle Woodland period, A.D. 1–400
Ohio Historical Society, Columbus 957/187
References: See Mills 1909, 1922
Plate 42

37
Horned-Monster-Effigy Boatstone
Stone; l. 24.6 cm, w. 8 cm
Mound 4, Turner site, Hamilton County, Ohio
Ohio Hopewell culture, Middle Woodland period, A.D. 200–400
Peabody Museum of Archaeology and Ethnology, Harvard University, Cambridge, Massachusetts 82-35-10/29685
Reference: Willoughby and Hooton 1922:63, pl. 19a–b
Plate 43

38
Bird-Head-Effigy Carving
Garnet-mica schist; h. 5.5 cm, l. 10.8 cm
Mound 1, Russell Brown mounds, Ross County, Ohio
Ohio Hopewell culture, Middle Woodland period, A.D. 100–300
Thomas Gilcrease Institute for American History and Art, Tulsa, Oklahoma 6124.20.133
Reference: Seeman and Soday 1980:79–80, fig. 5
Plate 44

39
Kneeling Male Figurine
Terra cotta; h. 8.3 cm, w. 3.7 cm
Mound 4, Turner site, Hamilton County, Ohio
Ohio Hopewell culture, Middle Woodland Period, A.D. 200–400
Peabody Museum of Archaeology and Ethnology, Harvard University, Cambridge, Massachusetts 82-35-10/29687
References: Willoughby and Hooton 1922: 71–74, pls. 20, 21e; Griffin et al. 1970: pls. 87, 88c
Plate 45

40
Coyote-Effigy Platform Pipe
Pipestone; h. 6.4 cm, l. 7 cm
Tremper mound, Scioto County, Ohio
Ohio Hopewell culture, Middle Woodland period, 200 B.C.–A.D. 100
Ohio Historical Society, Columbus 125/21
Reference: Mills 1916:303–304, fig. 20
Plate 46

41
Falcon-Effigy Platform Pipe
Pipestone, river pearl; h. 5.4 cm, l. 8.3 cm
Tremper mound, Scioto County, Ohio
Ohio Hopewell culture, Middle Woodland Period, 200 B.C.–A.D. 100
Ohio Historical Society, Columbus 125/19
Reference: Mills 1916: 329–330, fig. 46
Plate 47

42
Beaver-Effigy Platform Pipe
Pipestone, river pearl, bone; h. 4.5
    cm, l. 11.6 cm
Bedford mound, Pike County,
    Illinois
Havana culture, Middle Woodland
    period, 100 B.C.–A.D. 200
Excavated by Gregory Perino from
    Bedford mound, 1955
Thomas Gilcrease Institute of Ameri-
    can History and Art, Tulsa, Okla-
    homa 6124.1140
Reference: Morse 1956:157
Plate 48

43
Bear-Effigy Platform Pipe
Pipestone, copper; h. 5.6 cm, l. 8.8 cm
Wilson mound 6, White County,
    Illinois
Crab Orchard culture, Middle Wood-
    land period, 200 B.C.–A.D. 200
Southern Illinois University, Center
    for Archaeological Investigations,
    Carbondale 54.48/43
Reference: Neuman and Fowler
    1952: 205, pl. 6c
Plate 49

44
Cardinal-Effigy Platform Pipe
Red sandstone; h. 4.5 cm, l. 8.1 cm
Wilson mound 6, White County,
    Illinois
Crab Orchard culture, Middle Wood-
    land period, 200 B.C.–A.D. 200
Illinois State Museum of Natural His-
    tory and Art, Springfield 802211
Reference: Neuman and Fowler
    1952: 197, pl. 6b
Plate 50

45
Raven-Effigy Platform Pipe
Conglomerate; h. 6.2 cm, l. 12.2 cm
Rutherford mound, Hardin County,
    Illinois
Crab Orchard culture, Middle Wood-
    land period, 200 B.C.–A.D. 200
Illinois State Museum of Natural His-
    tory and Art, Springfield 814510
Reference: Fowler 1957: 17–18, pl. 5
Plate 51

46
Seated Human Figurine
Terra cotta; h. 2.5 cm, w. 1.5 cm
Smiling Dan site, Scott County,
    Illinois
Havana culture, Middle Woodland
    period, 50 B.C.–A.D. 250
Center for American Archeology,
    Kampsville, Illinois, and Illinois
    Department of Transportation,
    Springfield SMD SQ. 52-24D-7
Reference: Stafford and Sant 1983:
    613
Plate 52

47
Seated Male Figurine
Terra cotta; h. 8.4 cm, w. 3.5 cm
Carrier Mills site, Saline County,
    Illinois
Crab Orchard/Allison culture, Mid-
    dle Woodland period, A.D. 100–300
Southern Illinois University, Center
    for Archaeological Investigations,
    Carbondale
Reference: Jeffries and Butler 1982,
    I: 252, fig. 60, pl. 30
Plate 53

48
Seated Female Figurine
Terra cotta; h. 8.3 cm, w. 3.3 cm
Twenhofel site, Jackson County,
    Illinois
Havana culture, Middle Woodland
    period, A.D. 100–300
Illinois State Museum of Natural His-
    tory and Art, Springfield 803630
References: Smail 1954: 32–33, fig.
    22; Griffin et al. 1970: 83, pl. 86a
Plate 54

49
Human Figurine Fragment
Terra cotta; h. 4.7 cm, w. 3.2 cm
Twenhofel site, Jackson County,
    Illinois
Havana culture, Middle Woodland
    period, A.D. 100–300
Collected by Willie Smith, Murphys-
    buro, Illinois, 1950
Illinois State Museum of Natural His-
    tory and Art, Springfield 803631
Plate 55

50
Jar (Havana Zoned)
Terra cotta; h. 15.5 cm, diam. 15.3 cm
Mound 6, Havana mounds, Mason County, Illinois
Havana culture, Middle Woodland period, 200–100 B.C.
University of Illinois Museum of Natural History, Urbana A4805
References: Moorehead and Taylor 1928: 155–164: Baker et al. 1941: 16, pl. 11, fig. 2; McGregor 1952: 77, pls. 24a, 25a. See Griffin 1952b: 106
Plate 56

51
Jar (Hopewell Zoned Stamped)
Terra cotta; h. 14 cm, diam. 14.3 cm
Mound 7, Klunk mound group, Calhoun County, Illinois
Havana culture, Middle Woodland period, A.D. 1–200
Thomas Gilcrease Institute of American History and Art, Tulsa, Oklahoma 5424.4702
Reference: Perino 1968: 9–214 (esp. 87), fig. 14. See Griffin 1952b: 116
Plate 57

52
Jar (Hopewell Zoned Incised)
Terra cotta; h. 13.4 cm, diam. 16.4 cm
Madison or St. Clair County, Illinois
Havana culture, Middle Woodland period, A.D. 1–200
Ex-coll. Hilgard, Illinois; ex-coll. Missouri Historical Society, Columbus 599; ex-coll. Paul Titterington
University of Michigan Museum of Anthropology, Ann Arbor 45249/599
Reference: Holmes 1903: 193, pl. 169e. See Griffin 1952b: 118
Plate 58

53
Platform Pipe
Serpentine; h. 14.3 cm, l. 19.1 cm
Cattaraugus County, New York
Squakie Hill complex, Middle Woodland period, 200 B.C.–A.D. 400
Excavated by Melvin Fillmore, 1893
The Gordon Hart Collection, Bluffton, Indiana
Plate 59

54
Falcon-Effigy Pipe
Steatite; l. 19.9 cm
Adams County, Ohio
Copena culture, Middle Woodland period, A.D. 100–400
The Brooklyn Museum 69.84
Plate 60

55
Panther-Effigy Pipe
Steatite; h. 6 cm, l. 16 cm
Mann site, Posey County, Indiana
Allison/Copena culture, Middle Woodland period, A.D. 1–400
Pipe found by Henry Mann, 1916; right foreleg recovered, 1938
On loan to the Brooklyn Museum L49.5
Plate 61

56
Bird-and-Owl-Effigy Great Pipe
Steatite; h. 15.4 cm, l. 25.5 cm
Scott County, Virginia
Copena culture, Middle Woodland period, A.D. 100–600
The National Museum of Natural History, Smithsonian Institution, Washington, D.C. 211243
References: Kelemen 1943, II: pl. 295; Fundaburk and Foreman 1957: pl. 104
Plate 62

57
Owl-Effigy Tubular Pipe
Steatite; l. 25 cm, w. 12.6 cm
Trigg County, Kentucky
Copena culture, Middle Woodland period, A.D. 100–600
The Museum of the American Indian, Heye Foundation, New York 19/5117
Plate 63

58
Raven-Effigy Pipe
Stone; h. 16 cm, w. 9.3 cm
Gedde Island, Tennessee
Jersey Bluff culture, Late Woodland period, A.D. 400–900
Thomas Gilcrease Institute of American History and Art, Tulsa, Oklahoma 5125.1201
Plate 64

59
Platform Pipe
Steatite; h. 10.8 cm, l. 24.2 cm
Virginia
Late Woodland period, A.D. 600–900
Thomas Gilcrease Institute of American History and Art, Tulsa, Oklahoma 6124.1726
Plate 65

60.1–.3
Three Bird-Effigy Plummets
Stone; l. 9 cm; l. 10 cm; l. 9.5 cm
Florida
Deptford culture, Middle Woodland period, 400 B.C.–A.D. 1
The Brooklyn Museum 64.211.1–.3
Reference: See Lafond 1972:81–86
Plate 66

61
Zoned Jar (Alligator Bayou Stamped)
Ceramic; h. 13.7 cm, diam. 16.4 cm
Alligator Bayou, St. Andrews Bay, Washington County, Florida
Porter/Santa Rosa culture, Middle Woodland period, 100 B.C.–A.D. 400
The Museum of the American Indian, Heye Foundation, New York 17/3755
References: Moore 1902:151, fig. 35; Willey 1949b:372–373, fig. 22b; Sears 1962:12–13; Walthall 1979:205, fig. 26.4
Plate 67

62
Castellated Vessel (Weeden Island Incised)
Ceramic; h. 13.4 cm, diam. 16.5 cm
Fowler's Landing, Levy County, Florida
Weeden Island culture, Late Woodland period, A.D. 400–900
The Museum of the American Indian, Heye Foundation, New York 17/1459
References: Moore 1903:367, fig. 3; Willey 1949a:414, fig. 35c
Plate 68

63
Bird-Effigy Vessel
Ceramic; h. 33 cm, w. 22.9 cm
Kolomoki site, Early County, Georgia
Crystal River/Kolomoki culture, Middle Woodland period, A.D. 1–500

Kolomoki Mounds Museum [Blakely], Parks and Historic Sites Division, Georgia Department of Natural Resources, Atlanta
References: See Willey 1949b:409–411
Plate 69

64
Human-Effigy Urn
Ceramic; h. 36.4 cm, diam. 22.9 cm
Buck mound, Santa Rosa Sound, Okaloosa County, Florida
Weeden Island culture, Late Woodland period, A.D. 600–900
Temple Mound Museum, Fort Walton Beach, Florida 1197
References: Brose 1979a:147, fig. 19.2; Lazarus 1979:14–10, cover, figs. 4, 11–12, pl. 2
Plate 70

65
Charnel House Post with Eagle Effigy
Wood (head restored); h. 157 cm, w. 38.1 cm
Fort Center site, Glades County, Florida
Belle Glade culture, Late Woodland period, A.D. 500–1000
Florida State Museum, Gainesville 62355
References: Milanich and Fairbanks 1980:187, fig. 35; Sears 1982:8
Plate 71

66
Bowl with Two Bird-Head Adornos (Fort Walton Incised)
Ceramic; h. 17.7 cm, diam. 31.1 cm
Hogtown Bayou, Choctawhatchee Bay, Walton County, Florida
Fort Walton culture, Late Mississippian period, A.D. 1350–1500
The Museum of the American Indian, Heye Foundation, New York 6/2177
Reference: See Willey 1949a:460–462
Plate 72

67
Frog- or Fish-Effigy Bowl
Ceramic; h. 7 cm, diam. 16.5 cm
Site 8WL33, Choctawhatchee Bay,
Walton County, Florida
Fort Walton culture, Late Mississippian period, A.D. 1350–1500
Temple Mound Museum, Fort Walton Beach, Florida 1305
References: Lazarus and Hawkins 1976:61 (ill.). See also Willey 1949a:460–462
Plate 73

68
Marine-Shell-Effigy Bowl (Pensacola Incised)
Ceramic; h. 7.6 cm, diam. 29.2 cm
Site 8WL30, Choctawhatchee Bay,
Walton County, Florida
Fort Walton culture, Late Mississippian period, A.D. 1350–1500
Temple Mound Museum, Fort Walton Beach, Florida 1265
References: Lazarus and Hawkins 1976:22–23, 33 (ill.). See also Willey 1949a:464
Plate 74

69
Kneeling Feline Figure
Wood; h. 15.1 cm
Key Marco, Collier County, Florida
Calusa culture, Late Mississippian period, A.D. 1400–1500
The National Museum of Natural History, Smithsonian Institution, Washington, D.C. 240915
References: Cushing 1896:387, 429, pl. 35.1; Gilliland 1975:116, cover, pls. 69–71
Plate 75

70
Engraved Bottle (Haley Engraved)
Ceramic; h. 20.7 cm, diam. 13.5 cm
Battle Place site, Lafayette County, Arkansas
Haley phase, Caddoan culture, Mississippian period, A.D. 1200–1400
Ex-coll. N. P. Miroir, Texarkana
University of Arkansas Museum, Fayetteville 55-16-3
References: Suhm and Jelks 1962: pls. 31e and e'
Plate 76

71
Double Bottle (Hudson Engraved)
Ceramic; h. 15.8 cm, w. 20.3 cm
Podo Place, Fourche River, Yell County, Arkansas
Caddoan culture, Late Mississippian period, A.D. 1500–1800
Thomas Gilcrease Institute of American History and Art, Tulsa, Oklahoma 5424.1523
References: See Suhm and Jelks 1962: 81, pl. 41
Plate 77

72
Bottle (Baily Engraved)
Ceramic; h. 20.6 cm, diam. 16.8 cm
Mound near Maluern, Ouachita River, Hot Springs County, Arkansas
Caddoan culture, Mississippian period, A.D. 1200–1500
Excavated by R. W. Williams, 1922
Thomas Gilcrease Institute of American History and Art, Tulsa, Oklahoma 5425.252
Reference: See Suhm and Jelks 1962: 5–6
Plate 78

73
Tripod Bottle (Hodges Engraved)
Ceramic; h. 18.6 cm, diam. 14.8 cm
Kimes Place, Ouachita River, Garland County, Arkansas
Caddoan culture, Mississippian period, A.D. 1200–1500
Thomas Gilcrease Institute of American History and Art, Tulsa, Oklahoma 5425.629
Reference: See Suhm and Jelks 1962: 73–76
Plate 79

74
Seed Jar
Ceramic; h. 26.7 cm, diam. 14.7 cm
Saline River, Grant County, Arkansas
Caddoan culture, Late Mississippian period, A.D. 1300–1500
Thomas Gilcrease Institute of American History and Art, Tulsa, Oklahoma 5425.168
Plate 80

75
Bottle (Nashville Negative Painted)
Ceramic; h. 20 cm, diam. 16.4 cm
Scott County, Arkansas

Mississippian period, A.D. 1300–1500
Thomas Gilcrease Institute of American History and Art, Tulsa, Oklahoma 5425.69
References: See Phillips 1970:139–141
Plate 81

76
Bottle with Spiral Design (Nodena Red and White)
Ceramic; h. 19.8 cm, diam. 18.7 cm
Carden Bottom, Arkansas River, Yell County, Arkansas
Late Mississippian period, A.D. 1300–1500
Thomas Gilcrease Institute of American History and Art, Tulsa, Oklahoma 5424.1656
Reference: See Phillips 1970:141–144
Plate 82

77
Bottle with Spiral Design (Nodena Red and White)
Ceramic; h. 22.4 cm, diam. 16.6 cm
Chicot County, Arkansas
Late Mississippian period, A.D. 1300–1500
Thomas Gilcrease Institute of American History and Art, Tulsa, Oklahoma 5424.2559
Reference: See Phillips 1970:141–144
Plate 83

78
Turtle-Effigy Vessel (Avenue Polychrome)
Ceramic; h. 16.8 cm, diam. 22.6 cm
Marked Tree site, Poinsett County, Arkansas
Quapaw culture, Late Mississippian period, A.D. 1300–1500
University of Arkansas Museum, Fayetteville 47-36-40
Reference: See Phillips 1970:40–41
Plate 84

79
Dog-Effigy Vessel
Ceramic; h. 19.5 cm, l. 25.6 cm
Bud Medley Place, Bayou Maçon, Chicot County, Arkansas
Late Mississippian period, A.D. 1500

Thomas Gilcrease Institute of American History and Art, Tulsa, Oklahoma 5425.2559
Reference: See Phillips 1970:141–144
Plate 85

80
Bowl with Crested-Bird Adorno (Leland Incised)
Ceramic; diam. 22.3 cm
Sawyer's Landing site, Arkansas
Late Mississippian period, A.D. 1300–1500
The Museum of the American Indian, Heye Foundation, New York 17/4157
References: Moore 1908:511, fig. 27. See also Phillips 1970:104–107
Plate 86

81
Frog-Effigy Vessel (Bell Plain)
Ceramic; l. 29.2 cm
Mississippi County, Arkansas
Mississippian period, A.D. 1200–1500
Ex-coll. Dr. Henry M. Whelpley
St. Louis Museum of Science and Natural History 8X69
References: Blake and Houser 1978: pl. 16. See also Phillips 1970:58–61
Plate 87

82
Bear-Effigy Bottle
Ceramic; h. 18.7 cm, l. 20.7 cm
Arkansas or Tennessee
Mississippian period, A.D. 1200–1500
University of Arkansas Museum, Fayetteville, 47-6-225
Plate 88

83
Turtle-Effigy Vessel (Bell Plain)
Ceramic; h. 21.1 cm, l. 26 cm
Scott County, Missouri
Late Mississippian period, A.D. 1300–1500
Thomas Gilcrease Institute of American History and Art, Tulsa, Oklahoma 5425.72
References: Griffin 1952a: fig. 122K. See also Phillips 1970:58–61
Plate 89

84
Reclining-Human-Effigy Bowl
Ceramic; h. 12 cm, l. 22.5 cm, w.
15.5 cm
Mississippi County, Arkansas
Late Mississippian period, A.D. 1300–
1500
Ex-coll. Dr. Henry M. Whelpley
St. Louis Museum of Science and
Natural History 8X58
Reference: Blake and Houser 1978:
pl. 12
Plate 90

85
**Human-Head-Effigy Vessel (No-
dena Red and White)**
Ceramic; h. 15.6 cm, diam. 18.5 cm
Paducah area, McKracken County,
Kentucky
Late Mississippian period, A.D. 1300–
1500
Ex-coll. George Flannery, 1875–
1929; ex-coll. Carnegie Public
Library
The Museum of the American Indi-
an, Heye Foundation, New York
23/980
Reference: See Phillips 1970:141–144
Plate 91

86
**Human-Head-Effigy Vessel (No-
dena Red and White)**
Ceramic; h. 15.1 cm, diam. 18.1 cm
Matlock site, Mississippi County,
Arkansas
Late Mississippian period, A.D. 1300–
1500
University of Arkansas Museum,
Fayetteville 31-35-3
References: Phillips et al. 1951: fig.
11. See also Phillips 1970:141–144
Plate 92

87
Human-Head-Effigy Vessel
Ceramic; h. 19.1 cm
Fortune mound, Poinsett County,
Arkansas
Late Mississippian period, A.D. 1300–
1500
Collected by Edwinn Curtiss, 1880
Peabody Museum of Archaeology
and Ethnology, Harvard University
Cambridge, Massachusetts 80-20-
10/21542
Plate 93

88
Human-Head Effigy
Red cedar; h. 9.5 cm, w. 6.7 cm
Craig mound, Spiro site, LeFlore
County, Oklahoma
Spiro phase, Caddoan culture, Mis-
sissippian period, A.D. 1200–1350
Thomas Gilcrease Institute of Ameri-
can History and Art, Tulsa, Okla-
homa 7325.35
Reference: J. A. Brown 1976b:449,
fig. 88c
Plate 94

89
Seated Male Figurine
Wood; h. 18.7 cm, w. 7.7 cm
Craig mound, Spiro site, LeFlore
County, Oklahoma
Spiro phase, Caddoan culture, Mis-
sissippian period, A.D. 1200–1350
Thomas Gilcrease Institute of Ameri-
can History and Art, Tulsa, Okla-
homa 7325.3
Reference: J. A. Brown 1976b:450–
451, fig. 90
Plate 95

90
Seated Male Figurine
Wood, pigment; h. 32.5 cm, w. 16.8 cm
Craig mound, Spiro site, LeFlore
County, Oklahoma
Spiro phase, Caddoan culture, Mis-
sissippian period, A.D. 1200–1350
The National Museum of Natural
History, Smithsonian Institution,
Washington, D.C. 448892
Reference: Hamilton 1952: pl. 26
(right)
Plate 96

91
Chunkey-Player-Effigy Pipe
Bauxite; h. 20.9 cm, l. 12.8 cm, w.
10.5 cm
Arkansas River valley, Muskogee
County, Oklahoma
Caddoan culture, Mississippian peri-
od, A.D. 1200–1350
Found by F. S. Brochett, February 7,
1907; ex-coll. Dr. Henry M.
Whelpley
St. Louis Museum of Science and
Natural History 12X83
Plate 97

92
Big Boy (Effigy Pipe)
Bauxite; h. 27.5 cm, w. 23 cm
Spiro site, LeFlore County, Oklahoma
Spiro phase, Caddoan culture, Mississippian period, A.D. 1200–1350
University of Arkansas Museum, Fayetteville 47-2-1
References: Hamilton 1952:34–35, pls. 9–10; J. A. Brown 1976b: 256–258, fig. 53
Plate 98

93
Monolithic Ax
Stone; l. 33.7 cm, w. 16.2 cm
Spiro site, LeFlore County, Oklahoma
Spiro phase, Caddoan culture, Mississippian period, A.D. 1200–1350
Thomas Gilcrease Institute of American History and Art, Tulsa, Oklahoma 6125.18910
References: J. A. Brown 1976b:187, fig. 34a
Plate 99

94
Monolithic Ax
Stone; l. 36 cm, w. 16.8 cm
Spiro site, LeFlore County, Oklahoma
Spiro phase, Caddoan culture, Mississippian period, A.D. 1200–1350
Thomas Gilcrease Institute of American History and Art, Tulsa, Oklahoma 6125.1781
References: Hamilton 1952:46, pl. 56; J. A. Brown 1976b:189, fig, 34c
Plate 100

95
Repoussé Male Profile
Copper; h. 24 cm, w. 17.4 cm
Craig mound, Spiro site, LeFlore County, Oklahoma
Spiro phase, Caddoan culture, Mississippian period, A.D. 1200–1350
Ohio Historical Society, Columbus
References: Hamilton 1952:53, pl. 73; Hamilton et al. 1974:145–146, fig. 88; J. A. Brown 1976b: 418, 433–437
Plate 101

96
Engraved Shell Cup Showing Four Horned Serpents
Marine shell; l. 21.9 cm, w. 14 cm
Craig mound, Spiro site, LeFlore County, Oklahoma
Spiro phase, Caddoan culture, Mississippian period, A.D. 1200–1350
University of Arkansas Museum, Fayetteville 37-1-39
References: Hamilton 1952:70–71, pls. 111, 235; Howard 1968:55, fig. 16c; Phillips and Brown 1978:pl.229
Plate 102

97
Engraved Cup Fragment
Marine shell; h. 20 cm, w. 14.7 cm
Craig mound, Spiro site, LeFlore County, Oklahoma
Spiro phase, Caddoan culture, Mississippian period, A.D. 1200–1350
University of Arkansas Museum, Fayetteville 37-1-43
References: Hamilton 1952:78, pl. 133A; Howard 1968:55, fig. 16b; Phillips and Brown 1978:223
Plate 103

98
Bird-Head Effigy
Marine shell; h. 5.7 cm, l. 10.5 cm
Spiro site, LeFlore County, Oklahoma
Spiro phase, Caddoan culture, Mississippian period, A.D. 1200–1350
University of Arkansas Museum, Fayetteville 37-1-18
Plate 104

99
Engraved Pendant Showing a Pair of Hands
Marine shell; h. 8.4 cm, w. 8.6 cm
Craig mound, Spiro site, LeFlore County, Oklahoma
Spiro phase, Caddoan culture, Mississippian period, A.D. 1200–1350
Thomas Gilcrease Institute of American History and Art, Tulsa, Oklahoma 9025.451
References: Hamilton 1952: 57, 61, pls. 82d, 91c; Perino 1966:7, fig. 3
Plate 105

100

Nursing-Mother-Effigy Bottle
Ceramic; h. 14.9 cm, w. 9.7 cm
Cahokia area, St. Clair County,
  Illinois
Cahokia culture, Mississippian peri-
  od, A.D. 1200–1400
Ex-coll. Dr. Henry M. Whelpley
St. Louis Museum of Science and
  Natural History 8X65
Reference: Blake and Houser 1978:
  pl. 7
Plate 106

101

**Kneeling-Human-Effigy Bottle (Bell
Plain)**
Ceramic; h. 16 cm, w. 13.8 cm
Missouri or Arkansas
Late Mississippian period, A.D. 1300–
  1500
Thomas Gilcrease Institute of Ameri-
  can History and Art, Tulsa, Okla-
  homa 5425.1517
Reference: See Phillips 1970:58–61
Plate 107

102

Human-Effigy Vessel
Ceramic; h.22 cm, w. 14 cm
Charleston area, Mississippi County,
  Missouri
Mississippian period, A.D. 1100–1300
Ex-coll. Dr. Edward Palmer
The National Museum of Natural
  History, Smithsonian Institution,
  Washington, D.C. 71734
Plate 108

103

Bowl with Head Adorno (Bell Plain)
Ceramic; h. 10.8 cm, diam. 21 cm
Stoddard County, Missouri
Late Mississippian period, A.D. 1300–
  1500
Thomas Gilcrease Institute of Ameri-
  can History and Art, Tulsa, Okla-
  homa 5425.51
Reference: See Phillips 1970:58–61
Plate 109

104

Frog-Effigy Pipe
Bauxite; h. 13 cm, l. 16 cm, w. 10 cm
East St. Louis, St. Clair County,
  Illinois
Stirling phase, Cahokia culture, Late

Mississippian period, A.D. 1000–
  1300
Illinois State Museum of Natural His-
  tory and Art, Springfield 800519
References: MacAdams 1887: 46;
  Emerson 1982:33, figs. 19a–b
Plate 110

105

Human-Effigy Pipe
Bauxite; h. 19.3 cm, l. 18 cm
Piasa Creek mound, Madison Coun-
  ty, Illinois
Stirling phase, Cahokia culture, Late
  Mississippian period, A.D. 1000–
  1300
Thomas Gilcrease Institute of Ameri-
  can History and Art, Tulsa, Okla-
  homa 6124.18.913
References: MacAdams 1887:46;
  Perino 1971:119; Emerson 1982:
  13–14, fig. 7
Plate 111

106

Human-Effigy Pipe
Bauxite; h. 9.3 cm, l. 12.7 cm
Guy Smith Village site, Cahokia cul-
  ture, Late Mississippian period, A.D.
  1000–1300
University of Illinois Museum of Nat-
  ural History, Urbana A3419
References: West 1932, II:706; Em-
  erson 1982:15, fig. 8
Plate 112

107

Birger Figurine
Bauxite; h. 20 cm, w. 14 cm
BBB Motor site, near Collinsville,
  Madison County, Illinois
Stirling phase, Cahokia culture, Mis-
  sissippian period, A.D. 1000–1250
Illinois Archaeological Survey, Ur-
  bana, and Illinois Department of
  Transportation, Springfield
References: Emerson 1982:3–8, figs.
  3–4; Emerson and Jackson 1984:
  254–261, pls. 5–7
Plate 113

108

Keller Figurine
Bauxite; h. 13 cm, w. 7 cm, d. 9.7 cm
BBB Motor site, near Collinsville,
  Madison County, Illinois
Stirling phase, Cahokia culture, Mis-
  sissippian period, A.D. 1000–1250

Illinois Archaeological Survey, Urbana, and Illinois Department of Transportation, Springfield
References: Emerson 1982:3–8, fig. 5; Emerson and Jackson 1984: 254–261, pl.8
Plate 114

109.1–.3
Long-Nosed-God Ear Ornaments
Marine shell; h. 3.5 cm, w. 2.95 cm; h. 3.4 cm, w. 2.8 cm; h. 4.2 cm, w. 3.55 cm.
Booker T. Washington site, St. Clair County, Illinois
Cahokia culture, Mississippian period, A.D. 1100–1200
Thomas Gilcrease Institute of American History and Art, Tulsa, Oklahoma 9025.227; 9025.228; 9025. 450
Reference: Perino 1966:8, fig. 2
Plate 115

110
Repoussé Plaque Showing Dancing Figures
Copper, pigment; h. 15.5 cm, w. 16.5 cm
Bluff Lake area, Union County, Illinois
Mississippian period, A.D. 1100–1300
The National Museum of Natural History, Smithsonian Institution, Washington, D.C. 88142
References: Thomas 1894:161, fig. 85; Phillips and Brown 1978:175, fig. 228
Plate 116

111.1
Wulfing Plate (**Repoussé Plaque**)
Copper; h. 30 cm, w. 13.5 cm
Malden, Dunklin County, Missouri
Mississippian period, A.D. 1200–1400
Found by Ray Groomes while plowing on Baldwin Farm, 1906
Washington University Gallery of Art, St. Louis 3679
References: Fowke 1910:98, pl. 16; Watson 1950:17, fig. 3, pl. 3; Howard 1968:33, figs 4, 6; Waring 1968:figs. 5a, 11, 13d
Plate 117

111.2
Wulfing Plate (**Repoussé Plaque**)
Copper; h. 33.5 cm, w. 14.5 cm
Malden, Dunklin County, Missouri
Mississippian period, A.D. 1200–1400
Found by Ray Groomes while plowing on Baldwin Farm, 1906
Washington University Gallery of Art, St. Louis 3681
References: Fowke 1910:98, pl. 15; Watson 1950:25, fig. 5, pl. 5; Waring 1968:16, fig. 5b
Plate 118

111.3
Wulfing Plate (**Repoussé Plaque**)
Copper; h. 21.1 cm, w. 16.1 cm
Malden, Dunklin County, Missouri
Mississippian period, A.D. 1200–1400
Found by Ray Groomes while plowing on Baldwin Farm, 1906
Washington University Gallery of Art, St. Louis 3680
References: Fowke 1910:98, pl. 19; Watson 1950:21, fig. 4; Waring 1968:42, fig. 13c
Plate 119

111.4
Wulfing Plate (**Repoussé Plaque**)
Copper; h. 31.7 cm, w. 13 cm
Malden, Dunklin County, Missouri
Mississippian period, A.D. 1200–1400
Found by Ray Groomes while plowing on Baldwin Farm, 1906
Washington University Gallery of Art, St. Louis 3685
References: Fowke 1910:98, pl. 17; Watson 1950:33
Plate 120

112
Engraved Palette Stone
Stone; diam. 31.9 cm
Moundville, Hale County, Alabama
Moundville culture, Mississippian period, A.D. 1200–1500
University of Alabama Museum of Natural History, University
References: Moore 1905:136, fig. 7; Holmes 1906:104, 107, pl. 13b; Jones 1942:7; Howard 1968:30, fig. 4a; Waring 1968:15, fig. 4u; Phillips and Brown 1978:138, fig. 199. See also Walthall 1980:221–227
Plate 121

113
Engraved Palette Stone
Stone; diam. 22.1 cm
Moundville, Hale County, Alabama
Moundville phase, Moundville culture, Mississippian period, A.D. 1200–1500
Peabody Museum of Archaeology and Ethnology, Harvard University, Cambridge, Massachusetts 96-11-10/48122
References: Moore 1905:131–134, figs. 4–5; Phillips and Brown 1978:143, fig. 208
Plate 122

114
Engraved Pendant
Red slate; l. 9.8 cm, w. 3.8 cm
Moundville, Hale County, Alabama
Moundville culture, Mississippian period, A.D. 1200–1500
University of Alabama Museum of Natural History, University
References: Jones 1942:4. See also Walthall 1980:221–227
Plate 123

115
Beaker (Pensacola Engraved, var. Little Lagoon)
Ceramic (incising heightened with modern pigment); h. 11.5 cm
Moundville site, Hale County, Alabama
Mississippian period, A.D. 1200–1500
University of Alabama Museum of Natural History, University
References: Jones 1942:11; DeJarnette 1952: fig. 152; Steponaitis 1983:223, fig. 65p
Plate 124

116
Engraved Jar (Walls Engraved)
Ceramic; h. 17.5 cm, diam. 20.5 cm
Beck site, Crittenden County, Arkansas
Late Mississippian period, A.D. 1300–1600
University of Arkansas Museum, Fayetteville 30-2-471
References: Phillips et al. 1951: fig. 111g
Plate 125

117
Seated-Male-Effigy Pipe
Banded slate; h. 9.3 cm, w. 3.6 cm, d. 4.6 cm
Jackson Township, Wells County, Indiana
Mississippian period, A.D. 1100–1350
Found by Mr. Oscar Byall on his property, 1865
The Gordon Hart Collection, Bluffton, Indiana
Plate 126

118
Bird-Effigy Pipe
Stone; h. 12.1 cm, w. 6 cm
Spencer County, Indiana
Early Mississippian period, A.D. 900–1300
Found by Mr. Holland Evans, 1930
The Gordon Hart Collection, Bluffton, Indiana
Plate 127

119
Crouching-Human-Effigy Pipe
Sandstone; h. 9 cm, l. 15 cm
Bell Field site (9 Mu 10), Murray County, Georgia
Little Egypt/Barnett phase, Lamar culture, Late Mississippian period, A.D. 1400–1600
University of Georgia, Department of Anthropology, Athens
Plate 128

120
Seated-Human-Effigy Pipe
Hematitic stone; l. 7.9 cm
Bell site, Roane County, Tennessee
Dallas phase, Dallas culture, Late Mississippian period, A.D. 1300–1500
Recovered by University of Tennessee archaeologists during WPA-sponsored excavations in Tennessee Valley Authority's Watts Bar reservoir, 1935
Frank H. McClung Museum, University of Tennessee, Knoxville 13/51RE1
References: Lewis 1937:23; Chapman 1982: back cover
Plate 129

121

Feline-Effigy Pipe

Stone; h. 10.5 cm, l. 12.7 cm

Anderson Plantation, Crooked Bayou, Chicot County, Arkansas

Mississippian period, A.D. 1200–1500

Thomas Gilcrease Institute of American History and Art, Tulsa, Oklahoma 6125.1204

Reference: Perino 1965:107, fig. 83

Plate 130

122

Kneeling-Prisoner-Effigy Pipe

Stone; h. 12.2 cm, l. 17 cm, w. 8.5 cm

Emerald site (?), Clairborne County, Mississippi

Emerald phase, Natchez culture, Late Mississippian period, A.D. 1400–1500

Ex-coll. Baron Hyde de Neuville, Rio de Janeiro; Baron Alexander von Humboldt; New York Historical Society

The Brooklyn Museum 37.2802

References: Squier and Davis 1848: 249, fig. 149; Schoolcraft 1855: pl. 8b

Plate 131

123

Dog-Effigy Vessel

Ceramic; h. 22.9 cm, w. 13 cm, l. 22 cm

Cumberland River area, Tennessee

Late Mississippian period, A.D. 1300–1500

Collected by Edwinn Curtiss, 1878

Peabody Museum of Archaeology and Ethnology, Harvard University, Cambridge, Massachusetts 78-6-10/13998

Plate 132

124

Engraved Shell Gorget Showing Two Bird-Men

Marine shell; diam. 11.5 cm

Hixon site, Hamilton County, Tennessee

Dallas phase, Dallas culture, Late Mississippian period, A.D. 1300–1500

Recovered by University of Tennessee archaeologists during WPA-sponsored excavations in Tennes-

see Valley Authority's Chickamauga Reservoir, 1936

Frank H. McClung Museum, University of Tennessee, Knoxville 566/1HA3

References: Lewis 1937:23; Lewis and Kneberg 1941: pl. 3.3; idem 1946: cover; Kneberg 1952: fig. 109g; idem 1959:9, fig. 18; Waring 1968:45, fig. 14i; Howard 1968:42, fig. 11c; Phillips and Brown 1978:127, fig. 178; Chapman 1982:fig. 65

Plate 133

125

Engraved Gorget Showing a Winged Figure

Marine shell; diam. 14 cm

Etowah site, Bartow County, Georgia

Wibanks phase, Etowah culture, Mississippian period, A.D. 1200–1450

Etowah Mounds Archaeological Area [Cartersville], Parks and Historic Sites Division, Georgia Department of Natural Resources, Atlanta

References: Phillips and Brown 1978:127, fig. 177

Plate 134

126

Engraved Shell Gorget Showing a Spider Motif

Marine shell; diam. 10 cm

Hixon site, Hamilton County, Tennessee

Dallas phase, Dallas culture, Late Mississippian period, A.D. 1300–1500

Recovered by University of Tennessee archaeologists during WPA-sponsored excavations in Tennessee Valley Authority's Chickamauga Reservoir, 1936

Frank H. McClung Museum, University of Tennessee, Knoxville 507/1HA3

References: Lewis 1937:23; Lewis and Kneberg 1941: pl. 3.4; Kneberg 1952: fig. 109g; idem 1959:13, fig. 24; Howard 1968:58, fig. 18a; Chapman 1982: fig. 51

Plate 135

127
**Engraved Gorget Showing a Rat-
tlesnake**
Marine shell; h. 12.2 cm, w. 15.5 cm
McMahan mound, Sevier County,
Tennessee
Dallas culture, Mississippian period,
A.D. 1200–1400
The National Museum of Natural
History, Smithsonian Institution,
Washington, D.C. 62841
Reference: Holmes 1883: pl. 64, fig. 4
Plate 136

128
Engraved Weeping-Eye Mask
Marine shell; h. 15 cm, w. 11.2 cm
Little Egypt site, Murray County,
Georgia
Barnett phase, Lamar culture, Late
Mississippian period, A.D. 1500–
1600
University of Georgia, Department of
Anthropology, Athens
References: Hally et al. 1979:99–
101, 259
Plate 137

129
**Spaghetti-Style Engraved Shell
Gorget**
Marine shell; diam. 17.2 cm
Dallas site, Hamilton Country,
Tennessee
Dallas phase, Dallas culture, Late
Mississippian period, A.D. 1300–
1500
Recovered by University of Tennes-
see archaeologists during WPA-
sponsored excavations in Tennes-
see Valley Authority's Chicka-
mauga Reservoir, 1936
Frank H. McClung Museum, Univer-
sity of Tennessee, Knoxville 767/
8HA1
References: Lewis and Kneberg 1941:
pls. 2.2, 3.5; Kneberg 1959:19, fig.
34; Chapman 1982:34, fig. 57
Plate 138

130
Seated Male Figurine
Sandstone; h. 46.2 cm
Sellers Farm site, Wilson County,
Tennessee
Late Mississippian period, A.D. 1300–
1500
Found in December 1939
Frank H. McClung Museum, Univer-
sity of Tennessee, Knoxville 1/
1WI1
References: Lewis 1948:15 (ill.);
Kneberg 1952: fig. 108d; Chap-
man 1982: cover
Plate 139

131
Seated Male Figurine
Sandstone; h. 44.6 cm
Mound C, Etowah site, Bartow
County, Georgia
Wibanks phase, Etowah culture,
Mississippian period, A.D. 1200–
1450
Robert S. Peabody Foundation for
Archaeology, Phillips Academy,
Andover, Massachusetts
Reference: Moorehead 1932:29, figs.
3, 69a
Plate 140

132.1–.2
Seated Female and Male Figurines
Marble; h. 61 cm
Etowah site, Bartow County, Georgia
Wibanks phase, Etowah culture,
Mississippian period, A.D. 1200–
1450
Etowah Mounds Archaeological
Area [Cartersville], Parks and His-
toric Sites Division, Georgia De-
partment of Natural Resources,
Atlanta
References: Kelly and Larson 1957:
43, 40–41 (ill.); Larson 1971: 65,
fig. 5
Plate 141

BIBLIOGRAPHY

Anderson, Duane C.
1975 "A Long-nosed God Mask from the Northwest." *American Antiquity* 40:326–329.

Asch, David L.
1976 *The Middle Woodland Population of the Lower Illinois Valley: A Study of Paleodemographic Methods.* Evanston: Northwestern Archaeological Program.

————, et al.
1979 "Woodland Subsistence and Settlement in West Central Illinois." In *Hopewell Archaeology,* eds. D. S. Brose and N. Greber, 80–85. Kent: Kent State University Press.

Baker, Frank C., et al.
1941 "Contributions to the Archaeology of the Illinois River Valley." *American Philosophical Society, Transactions* 32 (1).

Barbeau, Marius C.
1952 "The Old World Dragon in America." In *Indian Tribes of Aboriginal America, Selected Papers of the 29th Congress of Americanists,* ed. S. Tax. New York: Cooper Square.

Bareis, Charles J., and William M. Gardener
1968 "Three Long-nosed God Masks from Western Illinois." *American Antiquity* 33:495–498.

Barnouw, Victor
1977 *Wisconsin Chippewa Myths and Tales and Their Relation to Chippewa Life.* Madison: University of Wisconsin Press.

Binford, Lewis R.
1971 "Mortuary Practices: Their study and their potential." In *Approaches to the Social Dimensions of Mortuary Practices,* ed. James A. Brown. *Society for American Archaeology, Memoirs* 25.

Black, Glenn A.
1967 *Angel Site: An archaeological, historical, and ethnological study.* 2 vols. Indianapolis: Indiana Historical Society.

Blake, Leonard W., and James G. Houser
1978 "The Whelpley Collection of Indian Artifacts." *Academy of Science of St. Louis, Transactions* 32 (1).

Bourne, Edward Gaylord, ed.
1904 *Narratives of the Career of Hernando de Soto.* 2 vols. New York: Trail Makers Series.

Braun, David P.
1979 "Illinois Hopewell Burial Practices and Social Organization: A

Re-examination of the Klunk-Gibson Mound Group." In *Hopewell Archaeology,* eds. D. S. Brose and N. Greber, 66–79. Kent: Kent State University Press.

Brose, David S.
1976 "An Historical and Archaeological Investigation of the Hopeton Earthworks, Ross County, Ohio." Report to the National Park Service (file GX-G115-6-0410), Midwest Archaeological Center, Lincoln.
1978 "The Late Prehistory of the Upper Great Lakes." In *Handbook of the North American Indians: Northeast,* vol. 15, ed. B. Trigger, 569–582. Washington, D.C.: Smithsonian Institution.
1979a "An Interpretation of Hopewellian Traits in Florida." In *Hopewell Archaeology,* eds. D. S. Brose and N. Greber, 141–149. Kent: Kent State University Press.
1979b "A Speculative Model of the Role of Exchange in the Prehistory of the Eastern Woodlands." In *Hopewell Archaeology,* eds. D. S. Brose and N. Greber, 3–8. Kent: Kent State University Press.

_____, and N'omi Greber, eds.
1979 *Hopewell Archaeology.* Kent: Kent State University Press.

_____, and George W. Percy
1974 "Weeden Island Ecology: Subsistence and village life in northwest Florida." Paper presented at 39th annual meeting of the Society for American Archaeology, Washington, D.C.

Brown, Calvin S.
1926 *The Archaeology of Mississippi.* University: University of Mississippi and the Mississippi Archaeological Society.

Brown, James A.
1975 "Spiro Art and its Mortuary Contexts." In *Death and the Afterlife in Pre-Columbian America,* ed. Elizabeth P. Benson, 1–32. Washington, D.C.: Dumbarton Oaks Research Library and Collections.
1976a "The Southern Cult Reconsidered." *Midcontinental Journal of Archaeology* 1:115–135.
1976b *Spiro Studies: Vol. 4, The artifacts.* Third Annual Report of Caddoan Archaeology—Spiro Focus Research, pt. 2. Norman: University of Oklahoma Research Institute.
1979 "Charnel Houses and Mortuary Crypts: Disposal of the dead in the Middle Woodland period." In *Hopewell Archaeology,* eds. D. S. Brose and N. Greber, 211–219. Kent: Kent State University Press.
1980 "The Falcon and the Serpent: Style provinces in the Mississippian Southeast." Paper presented at 37th annual meeting of the Southeastern Archaeological Conference, New Orleans.
1983 "Rank and Warfare in Mississippian Period Art." Paper presented at 40th annual meeting of the Southeastern Archaeological Conference, Columbia.
1984 "Arkansas Valley Caddoan: The Spiro phase." In *Prehistory of Oklahoma,* ed. Robert E. Bell, 241–263. New York: Academic Press.

Buikstra, Jane
1976 *Hopewell in the Lower Illinois Valley: A regional study of human biological variability and prehistoric mortuary behavior.* Scientific Papers 2. Ev-

anston: Northwestern Archaeological Program.
1979 "Contributions of Physical Anthropology to the Concept of Hopewell: A historical perspective." In *Hopewell Archaeology*, eds. D. S. Brose and N. Greber, 220–223. Kent: Kent State University Press.

Burnett, E. K.
1945 "The Spiro Mound Collection in the Museum." *Contributions from the Museum of the American Indian, Heye Foundation*, vol. 14.

Byers, Douglas S.
1962 "The Restoration and Preservation of Some Objects from Etowah." *American Antiquity* 28:206–216.

Cabeza de Vaca, Alvar Nuñez
1904 *The Journey of Alvar Nuñez Cabeza de Vaca*, ed. A. F. Bandelier. New York: Allerton Book Co.

Caldwell, Joseph R.
1964 "Interaction Spheres in Prehistory," In *Hopewellian Studies*, eds. J. R. Caldwell and R. L. Hall, 133–143. Scientific Papers 12. Springfield: Illinois State Museum.

———, **and Robert L. Hall, eds.**
1964 *Hopewellian Studies*. Scientific Papers 12. Springfield: Illinois State Museum.

Central States Archaeological Journal
1960 *Central States Archaeological Journal* 7 (1):29.

Chapman, Jefferson
1982 *The American Indian in Tennessee: An Archaeological Perspective*. Knoxville: The Frank H. McClung Museum and Department of Anthropology, University of Tennessee.

———, **and Bennie C. Keel**
1979 "Candy Creek-Connestee Components in Eastern Tennessee and Western North Carolina and Their Relationship with Adena-Hopewell." In *Hopewell Archaeology*, eds. D. S. Brose and N. Greber, 157–161. Kent: Kent State University Press.

Cole, Fay-Cooper, and Thorne Deuel
1937 *Rediscovering Illinois*. Chicago: University of Chicago Publications in Anthropology.

Conard, Nicholas, et al.
1984 "Accelerator Radiocarbon Dating of Evidence for Prehistoric Horticulture in Illinois." *Nature* 308:443–446.

Cunningham, Wilber M.
1948 "A Study of Glacial Kame Culture in Michigan, Ohio and Indiana." *University of Michigan Museum of Anthropology, Occasional Contributions* 12.

Cushing, Frank H.
1897 "Exploration of Ancient Key Dweller Remains on the Gulf Coast of Florida." *American Philosophical Society Proceedings* 25 (153).

Dalton, George
1977 "Aboriginal Economies in Stateless Societies." In *Exchange Sys-*

tems in Prehistory, eds. T. Y. Earle and J. E. Ericson. New York: Academic Press.

DeJarnette, D. L.
1952 "Alabama Archaeology: A summary." In *Archaeology of the Eastern United States*, ed. J. B. Griffin, 272–284. Chicago: University of Chicago Press.

Densmore, Frances
1929 "Chippewa Customs." *Bureau of American Ethnology Bulletin* 86.

Didier, Mary Ellen
1967 "A Distributional Study of the Turkey-Tail Point." *The Wisconsin Archaeologist* 48 (1):3–73.

Dragoo, Don, and Charles Wray
1964 "Hopewellian Figurine Rediscovered." *American Antiquity* 30:195–199.

Duffield, Lathiel F.
1964 "Engraved Shells from the Craig Mound, LeFlore County, Oklahoma." *Oklahoma Anthropological Society Memoirs* 1.

Emerson, Thomas E.
1982 *Mississippian Stone Images in Illinois.* Circular no. 6. Urbana: Illinois Archaeological Survey.

_____, and D.Y. Jackson
1984 "The BBB Motor Site: An Early Mississippian occupation." *University of Illinois FA1–270 Archaeological Mitigation Project Report 38.*

Fitting, James E.
1975 *The Archaeology of Michigan.* Bloomfield Hills: The Cranbrook Academy of Science.
1979 "Middle Woodland Cultural Development in the Straits of Mackinac Region: Beyond the Hopewell frontier." In *Hopewell Archaeology,* eds. D.S. Brose and N. Greber, 109–112. Kent: Kent State University Press.

_____, ed.
1972 "The Schutz Site at Green Point: A stratified occupation area in the Saginaw valley of Michigan." *University of Michigan Museum of Anthropology, Memoirs* 4.

Fogel, Ira L.
1963 "The Dispersal of Copper Artifacts in the Late Archaic Period of Prehistoric North America." *The Wisconsin Archaeologist* 44 (3): 129–179.

Ford, James A., and George J. Quimby
1945 "The Tchefuncte Culture: An occupation of the lower Mississippi valley." *Society for American Archaeology, Memoirs* 10 (3).

_____, and Clarence H. Webb
1956 "Poverty Point: A Late Archaic Site in Louisiana." *American Museum of Natural History, Anthropological Papers* 46, pt. 1.

_____, and Gordon R. Willey
1941 "An Interpretation of the Prehistory of the Eastern United States." *American Anthropologist* 43 (3): 325–363.

Fowke, Gerald
1910 "Antiquities of Central and Southeastern Missouri." *Bureau of American Ethnology Bulletin* 37.

Fowler, Melvin L.
1957 *Rutherford Mound, Hardin County, Illinois.* Scientific Papers 7 (1). Springfield: Illinois State Museum.
1969 "Exploration into Cahokia Archaeology." *Illinois Archaeological Survey, Bulletin* 7:1–30.
1974 "Cahokia: Ancient capital of the Midwest." *Addison-Wesley Module in Anthropology* 48.
1978 "Cahokia and the American Bottom: Settlement archaeology." In *Mississippian Settlement Patterns,* ed. Bruce D. Smith, 455–478. New York: Academic Press.

Fundaburk, Emma Lila, and Mary Douglass Fundaburk Foreman, eds.
1957 *Sun Circles and Human Hands, The Southeastern Indians—Art and Industries.* Luverne: Emma Lila Fundaburk.

Garcilaso de la Vega, G.S.
1951 *The Florida of the Inca.* Trans. and ed. J.G. Varner and J. J. Varner. Austin: University of Texas Press.

Gibson, Jon L.
1980 "Speculations on the Origin and Development of Poverty Point Culture." *Louisiana Archaeology* 6:319–348.
1983 *Poverty Point: A Culture of the Lower Mississippi Valley.* Anthropological Study no. 7. Baton Rouge: Louisiana Archaeological Survey of Antiquities Commission.

Gilliland, Marion S.
1975 *The Material Culture of Key Marco Florida.* Gainesville: University of Florida Press.

Goad, Sharon
1978 "Exchange Networks in the Prehistoric Southeastern United States." Ph.D. diss., University of Georgia. Ann Arbor: University Microfilms International.

Goggin, John M., and William C. Sturtevant
1964 "The Calusa: A stratified, nonagricultural society (With notes on sibling marriage)." In *Explorations in Cultural Anthropology: Essays in honor of George Peter Murdock,* ed. Ward H. Goodenough, 179–219. New York: McGraw-Hill Book Company.

Greber, N'omi
1976 "Within Ohio Hopewell: Analysis of burial patterns from several classic sites." Ph.D. diss., Case Western Reserve University. Ann Arbor: University Microfilms International.
1983 "Recent Excavations at the Edwin Harness Mound, Liberty Works, Ross County, Ohio." *Kirtlandia* 39.

Greenman, G.F.
1932 "Excavation of the Coon Mound and Analysis of Adena Culture." *Ohio Archaeological and Historical Quarterly* 41: 366–523.

Griffin, James B.
1952a "Prehistoric Cultures of the Central Mississippi Valley." In *Archaeology of the Eastern United States*, ed. J. B. Griffin, 226–238. Chicago: University of Chicago Press.
1952b "Some Early and Middle Woodland Pottery Types in Illinois." In *Hopewellian Communities in Illinois*, ed. T. Deuel, 93–130. Scientific Papers 5. Springfield: Illinois State Museum.
1952c "Culture Periods in Eastern United States Archaeology." In *Archaeology of the Eastern United States*, ed. J. B. Griffin. Chicago: University of Chicago Press.
1967 "Eastern North American Archaeology: A summary." *Science* 156:175–191.

———, et al.
1970 "The Burial Complexes of the Knight and Norton Mounds in Illinois and Michigan." *University of Michigan Museum of Anthropology, Memoirs* 2.
1978 "Late Prehistory of the Ohio Valley." In *Handbook of the North American Indians: Northeast*, vol. 15, ed. B. Trigger, 547–559. Washington, D.C.: Smithsonian Institution.

Hall, Robert L.
1983 "Long-distance Connections of Some Long-Nosed Gods." Paper presented at 82nd annual meeting of the American Anthropological Association, Chicago, Illinois.

Hally, David, et al.
1979 *Archaeological Investigation of the Little Egypt Site (9Mu102), Murray County, Georgia, 1969 Season*. Series Report no. 18. Athens: University of Georgia Laboratory of Archaeology.

Hamilton, Henry W.
1952 "The Spiro Mound." *Missouri Archaeologist* 14.

———, et al.
1974 "Spiro Mound Copper." *Missouri Archaeological Society, Memoirs* 11.

Harn, Alan D.
1974 "Another Long-nosed God Mask from Fulton County, Illinois." *The Wisconsin Archaeologist* 56:2–8.

Hatch, James Willis
1974 "Social Dimensions of Dallas Mortuary Patterns." Unpub. master's thesis, Pennsylvania State University.

Hertz, Robert
1960 *Death and the Right Hand*. New York: Free Press.

Holmes, William H.
1883 "Art in Shell of the Ancient Americans." *2nd Annual Report of the Bureau of American Ethnology*:185–305.
1903 "Aboriginal Pottery of the Eastern United States." *20th Annual Report of the Bureau of American Ethnology*:1–237.
1906 "Certain Notched or Scalloped Stone Tablets of the Moundbuilders." *American Anthropologist* n.s. 8:101–108.

Howard, James H.
1953 "The Southern Cult on the Northern Plains." *American Antiquity* 19 (2):38–39.
1956 "The Persistence of Southern Cult Gorgets Among the Historic Kansa." *American Antiquity* 21:301–303.
1968 "The Southeastern Ceremonial Complex and Its Interpretation." *Missouri Archaeological Society, Memoirs* 6.

Hudson, Charles
1976 *The Southeastern Indians.* Knoxville: The University of Tennessee Press.

Jeffries, Richard W.
1976 "The Tunacunnhee Site: Evidence of Hopewell interaction in northwest Georgia." *University of Georgia Anthropological Papers* 1.

————, and Brian M. Butler
1982 *The Carrier Mills Archaeological Project: Human adaptation in the Saline valley, Illinois.* Center for Archaeological Investigations, Research Paper 33. Carbondale: Southern Illinois University.

Jenkins, Ned J.
1981 "Archaeological Investigations in the Gainsville Lake of the Tennessee-Tombigbee Waterway: Ceramic description and chronology." *University of Alabama Office of Archaeological Research, Report of Investigations,* 12, pt. 2.

Jones, Walter Bryan
1942 "Mound State Monument, Moundville, Alabama." *Alabama Museum of Natural History, Papers* 20:3–19.

Kelemen, Pal
1943 *Medieval American Art.* 2 vols. New York: MacMillan Co.

Kellar, James H.
1979 "The Mann Site and 'Hopewell' in the Lower Wabash-Ohio Valley." In *Hopewell Archaeology,* eds. D. S. Brose and N. Greber, 100–107. Kent: Kent State University Press.

Kneberg, Madeline
1952 "The Tennessee Area." In *Archaeology of the Eastern United States,* ed. J. B. Griffin, 190–198. Chicago: University of Chicago Press.
1959 "Engraved Shell Gorgets and Their Associations." *Tennessee Archaeologist* 15:1–39.

Knoblock, Byron W.
1939 *Bannerstones of the North American Indian.* Lagrange: Byron W. Knoblock.

Krieger, Alex D.
1945 "An Inquiry into the Supposed Mexican Influence on a Prehistoric 'Cult' in the Southern United States." *American Anthropologist* 47: 483–515.

Lafond, Arthur A.
1972 "A Unique Zoormorphic Effigy from the Queen Mound, Jacksonville, Florida." *Florida Anthropologist* 25: 81–86.

Larson, Lewis H., Jr.
1971 "Archaeological Implications of Social Stratification at the Etowah Site, Georgia." In *Approaches to the Social Dimensions of Mortuary Practices,* ed. James A. Brown, 58–67. *Society for American Archaeology, Memoirs* 25.

_____, and A. R. Kelly
1957 "Explorations at Etowah, Georgia, 1954-1956." *Archaeology* 10(1): 39–48.

Lazarus, Yulee W.
1979 *The Buck Burial Mound: A mound of the Weeden Island culture.* Fort Walton Beach: Temple Mound Museum.

_____, and Carolyn B. Hawkins
1976 *Pottery of the Fort Walton Period.* Fort Walton Beach: Temple Mound Museum.

Le Page Du Pratz, Antoine S.
1758 *Histoire de la Louisiane.* 3 vols. Paris: De Bure, Sr.

Lewis, T. M. N.
1937 "Annotations Pertaining to Prehistoric Research in Tennessee." *University of Tennessee Record* 40 (6):3–28.
1948 "Stone Images." *Tennessee Archaeologist* 4: 14–15.

_____, and Madeline Kneberg
1941 *The Prehistory of the Chickamauga Basin in Tennessee: A Preview.* Tennessee Anthropology Papers 1. Knoxville: University of Tennessee.

_____, and Madeline Kneberg
1959 "The Archaic in the Middle South." *American Antiquity* 25 (2): 161–183.

Lorant, Stephan
1946 *The New World: The first pictures of America.* New York: Duell, Sloan and Pearce. 2nd ed. 1965.

MacAdams, W.
1887 *Records of Ancient Races in the Mississippi Valley.* St. Louis: C. R. Bornes.

MacCurdy, George G.
1913 "Shell Gorgets from Missouri." *American Anthropologist* n.s. 15: 395–414.

MacLeod, William Christie
1982 "Priests, Temples, and the Practice of Mummification in Southeastern North America." *Atti del XXII Congresso Internazionale degli Americanisti* 2: 207–230.

Madden, Betty I.
1974 *Art, Crafts, and Architecture in Early Illinois.* Urbana: University of Illinois Press.

Mainfort, Robert L., Jr.
1983 "Excavations at the Twin Mounds, Pinson Site." Paper presented at 40th annual Southeastern Archaeological Conference, Columbia, South Carolina.

Mason, Ronald
1981   *Great Lakes Archaeology.* New York: Academic Press.

McGregor, John C.
1952   "The Havana Site." In *Hopewellian Communities in Illinois,* ed. T. Deuel, 44–91. Scientific Papers 5. Springfield: Illinois State Museum.

McHugh, William P.
1973   "'New Archaeology' and the Old Copper Culture." *The Wisconsin Archaeologist* 54 (2): 70–83.

McKern, W. C., et al.
1945   "Painted Pottery Figures from Illinois." *American Antiquity* 10 (3): 295–302.

Milanich, Jerald T., and Charles H. Fairbanks
1980   *Florida Archaeology.* New York: Academic Press.

Mills, William C.
1909   "Explorations of the Seip Mound." *Ohio Archaeological and Historical Quarterly* 18: 113–193.
1916   "Exploration of the Tremper Mound." *Ohio Archaeological and Historical Quarterly* 25: 262–398.
1922   "Exploration of the Mound City Group." *Ohio Archaeological and Historical Quarterly* 31: 423–584.

Mooney, James
1900   "Myths of the Cherokee." *19th Annual Report of the Bureau of American Ethnology,* pt. 1:3–548.

Moore, Clarence B.
1902   "Certain Aboriginal Remains of the Northwest Florida Coast." *Journal of the Academy of Natural Sciences of Philadelphia* 12, pt. 2:127–355.
1903   "Certain Aboriginal Mounds of the Florida Central West Coast." *Journal of the Academy of Natural Sciences of Philadelphia* 12:361–492.
1905   "Certain Aboriginal Remains of the Black Warrior River." *Journal of the Academy of Natural Sciences of Philadelphia* 13:125–244.
1908   "Certain Mounds of Arkansas and of Mississippi." *Journal of the Academy of Natural Sciences of Philadelphia* 13:481–605.
1915   "Aboriginal Sites on the Tennessee River." *Journal of the Academy of Natural Sciences of Philadelphia* 16:170–428.
1916   "Some Aboriginal Sites on the Green River, Kentucky; Certain Aboriginal Sites on the Lower Ohio River. Additional Investigations on the Mississippi River." *Journal of the Academy of Natural Sciences of Philadelphia* 16, pt. 3:431–511.

Moorehead, Warren K.
1910   *The Stone Age of North America.* 2 vols. Boston: Houghton and Mifflin.
1917   *Stone Ornaments Used by the Indians of the United States and Canada.* Andover: Andover Press.
1922   "The Hopewell Mound Group of Ohio." *Field Museum of Natural History Publications* 9 (5):73–181.
1932   "Exploration of the Etowah Site in Georgia." *Etowah Papers.* New Haven: Yale University Press.

_____, and Jay L. B. Taylor
1928 "The Cahokia Mounds." *University of Illinois Bulletin* 26 (4).

Morse, Dan, M. D.
1956 "The Bedford Mound Beaver Monitor Pipe." *Central States Archaeological Journal* 2 (4):157.

Morse, Dan F., and Phyllis A. Morse
1983 *Archaeology of the Central Mississippi Valley.* New York: Academic Press.

Muller, Jon D.
1966 "An Experimental Theory of Stylistic Analysis." Unpub. Ph.D. diss., Harvard University.
1979 "Structural Studies of Art Styles." In *The Visual Arts, Plastic and Graphic*, ed. Justine Cordwell, 139–211. The Hague: Mouton.

Neitzel, Robert S.
1965 "Archaeology of the Fatherland Site: The grand village of the Natchez." *American Museum of Natural History, Anthropological Papers* 51, pt. 1.

Neuman, Georg K., and Melvin L. Fowler
1952 "Hopewellian Communities in the Wabash Valley." In *Hopewellian Communities in Illinois*, ed. T. Deuel, 175–248. Scientific Papers 5. Springfield: Illinois State Museum.

Otto, Martha Potter
1971 "Adena Culture Content and Settlement." In *Adena: The Seeking of an Identity*, ed. B. K. Swartz, Jr., 4–11. Muncie: Ball State University.
1975 "A New Engraved Adena Tablet." *Ohio Archaeologist* 25 (2):31–36.
1979 "Hopewell Antecedents in the Adena Heartland." In *Hopewell Archaeology*, eds. D. S. Brose and N. Greber, 9–14. Kent: Kent State University Press.

Peebles, Christopher S.
1971 "Moundville and Surrounding Sites; some structural considerations of mortuary practices." In *Approaches to the Social Dimensions of Mortuary Practices*, ed. James A. Brown, 68–91. *Society for American Archaeology, Memoirs* 25.
1978 "Determinants of Settlement Size and Location in the Moundville Phase." In *Mississippian Settlement Patterns*, ed. Bruce D. Smith, 369–416. New York: Academic Press.

_____, and S. M. Kus
1977 "Some Archaeological Correlates of Ranked Societies." *American Antiquity* 42 (3):421–448.

Penman, John T.
1977 "Old Copper Culture: An analysis of old copper artifacts." *The Wisconsin Archaeologist* 58 (1):3–23.

Penney, David W.
1980 "The Adena Engraved Tablets: A study of art prehistory." *Midcontinental Journal of Archaeology* 5 (1):3–38.

Perino, Gregory
1965 "Three Late Mississippian Effigy Pipes." *Central States Archaeological Journal* 12 (3):104–107.

1966   "Short History of Some Shell Ornaments." *Central States Archaeological Journal* 13 (1):560–563.
1968   "The Pete Klunk Mound Group, Calhoun County." *Illinois Archaeology Survey, Bulletin* 6:9–124.
1971   "The Mississippian Component of the Schild Site (No. 4), Green County, Illinois." In *Mississippian Site Archaeology in Illinois. I. Site Reports from the St. Louis and Chicago Areas. Illinois Archaeological Survey, Bulletin* 8:1–148.

Perttula, Timothy K., et al.
1982   "A Consideration of Caddoan Subsistence." *Southeastern Archaeology* 1:89–102.

Phillips, Philip
1970   "Archaeological Survey in the Lower Yazoo Basin, Mississippi, 1949–1955." *Peabody Museum of Archaeology and Ethnology, Harvard University, Papers* 60.

————, and James A. Brown
1978   *Pre-Columbian Shell Engravings from the Craig Mound at Spiro, Oklahoma*, pt. 1. Cambridge, Mass.: Peabody Museum of Archaeology and Ethnology, Harvard University.

————, and James A. Brown
1983   *Pre-Columbian Shell Engravings from the Craig Mound at Spiro, Oklahoma*, pt. 2. Cambridge, Mass.: Peabody Museum of Archaeology and Ethnology, Harvard University.

————, et al.
1951   "Archaeological Survey in the Lower Mississippi Valley, 1940–1947." *Peabody Museum of Archaeology and Ethnology, Harvard University, Papers* 25.

Ritzenthaler, Robert E., and George J. Quimby
1962   "The Red Ocher Culture of the Upper Great Lakes and Adjacent Areas." *Fieldiana Anthropology* 36:243–275.

Roper, Donna C.
1978   *The Airport Site: A multicomponent site in the Sangamon River drainage.* Illinois State Museum Research Series Papers in Anthropology, no. 4. Springfield: Illinois State Museum.

Schnell, Frank T., et al.
1981   *Chemochechobee: Archaeology of a Mississippi ceremonial center on the Chattahoochee River.* Gainesville: University Presses of Florida.

Schoolcraft, Henry R.
1855   *Information Respecting the History, Condition and Prospects of the Indian Tribes of the United States*, vol. 5. Philadelphia: J. B. Lippincott and Co.

Sears, William H.
1962   "The Hopewellian Affiliations of Certain Sites on the Gulf Coast of Florida." *American Antiquity* 28 (1):5–18.
1977   "Prehistoric Culture Areas and Culture Change on the Gulf Coastal Plain." In *For the Director: Research essays in honor of James B. Griffin*, ed. C. E. Cleland. *University of Michigan Museum of Anthropology, Anthropological Papers* 61.

1982 *Fort Center: An archaeological site in the Lake Okeechobee basin.* Gainesville: University Presses of Florida.

Seeman, Mark F., and Frank Soday
1980 "The Russell Brown Mounds: Three Hopewell Mounds in Ross County, Ohio." *Midcontinental Journal of Archaeology* 5 (1):73–116.

Shetrone, Henry C.
1926 "Explorations of the Hopewell Group of Prehistoric Earthworks." *Ohio Archaeological and Historical Quarterly* 35 (1):5–227.
1930 *The Moundbuilders.* New York: Appleton-Century.

_____, and G. F. Greenman
1931 "Exploration of the Seip Group of Prehistoric Earthworks." *Ohio Archaeological and Historical Quarterly* 40:349–509.

Skinner, Alanson
1915 "Societies of the Iowa, Kansa, and Ponca Indians." *Anthropological Paper of the American Museum of Natural History* 11, pt. 9.

Smail, William
1954 "A Hopewell Figurine." *Central States Archaeological Journal* (1):31–32.

Smith, Bruce D.
1978 "Variation in Mississippian Settlement Patterns." In *Mississippian Settlement Patterns,* ed. Bruce D. Smith, 479–503. New York: Academic Press.

Snyder, John Francis
1962 "Certain Indian Mounds Technically Considered." In *John Francis Snyder: Selected writings,* ed. C. C. Walton, 230–274. Springfield: Illinois Historical Society.

Spence, Michael, et al.
1979 "Hopewell Influences on Middle Woodland Cultures in Southern Ontario." In *Hopewell Archaeology,* eds. D. S. Brose and N. Greber, 115–121. Kent: Kent State University Press.

Spinden, Herbert J.
1913 "A Study of Maya Art." *Peabody Museum, Harvard University, Memoirs* 6.

Squier, G. E., and E. H. Davis
1848 "Ancient Monuments of the Mississippi Valley." *Smithsonian Contributions to Knowledge* 1.

Stafford, Barbara D., and Mark B. Sant
1983 *Excavations at the Smiling Dan Site: Delineation of site structure and function during the Middle Woodland period.* Evanston: The Center for American Archaeology and the Illinois Department of Transportation.

Steponaitis, Vincas P.
1983 *Ceramics, Chronology, and Community Patterns: An archaeological study at Moundville.* New York: Academic Press.

Stoltman, James B.
1974 "Groton Plantation: An Archaeological Study of a South Carolina Locality." *Monographs of the Peabody Museum,* no. 1. Cambridge, Mass.: Harvard University.

Suhm, Dee Ann, and Edward B. Jelks, eds.
1962   *Handbook of Texas Archaeology: Type descriptions.* Austin: The Texas Archaeological Society and the Texas Memorial Museum.

Swanton, John R.
1911   "Indian Tribes of the Lower Mississippi Valley and the Adjacent Gulf of Mexico." *Bureau of American Ethnology Bulletin* 43.
1928   "Religious Beliefs and Medical Practices of the Creek Indians." *42nd Annual Report of the Bureau of American Ethnology:* 473–672.
1931   "Source Material for the Social and Ceremonial Life of the Choctaw Indians." *Bureau of American Ethnology Bulletin* 103.
1946   "The Indians of the Southeastern United States." *Bureau of American Ethnology Bulletin* 137.

Sylvester, J. E.
1879   "Description of an Engraved Stone Found near Berlin, Jackson County, Ohio." *American Antiquarian and Oriental Journal* 1: 73–75.

Temple, Wayne C.
1956   "The Piasa Bird: Fact or fiction?" *Journal of the Illinois State Historical Society* 49: 308–322.

Thomas, Cyrus
1894   "Report of the Mound Explorations of the Bureau of American Ethnology." *12th Annual Report of the Bureau of American Ethnology.*

Thwaites, Reuben Gold, ed.
1896–1901   *The Jesuit Relations and Allied Documents.* 73 vols. Cleveland: Burrows Bros. Co.

Toth, Alan
1974   "Archaeology and Ceramics at the Marksville Site." *University of Michigan Museum of Anthropology, Anthropological Papers* 56.
1979   "The Marksville Connection." In *Hopewell Archaeology,* eds. D. S. Brose and N. Greber, 188–199. Kent: Kent State University Press.

Townsend, Earl G.
1959   *Birdstones of the North American Indian.* Indianapolis: Earl G. Townsend.

Tuck, James A.
1978   "Regional Cultural Development, 3000 to 300 B.C." In *Handbook of the North American Indians: Northeast,* vol. 15, ed. B. Trigger, 28–43. Washington, D.C.: Smithsonian Institution.

Turner, Victor W.
1974   *Dramas, Fields and Metaphors: Symbolic action in human society.* Ithaca: Cornell University Press.

Underhill, Ruth
1965   *Red Man's Religion.* Chicago: University of Chicago Press.

Walthall, John A.
1973   "Copena: A Tennessee valley Middle Woodland culture." Ph.D. diss., University of North Carolina. Ann Arbor: University Microfilms International.
1979   "Hopewell and the Southern Heartland." In *Hopewell Archaeology,* eds. D. S. Brose and N. Greber, 200–208. Kent: Kent State University Press.

1980 *Prehistoric Indians of the Southeast: Archaeology of Alabama and the Middle South.* University: University of Alabama Press.

Waring, Antonio J., Jr.
1968 "The Southern Cult and Muskhogean Ceremonial." In *The Waring Papers: The collected works of Antonio J. Waring, Jr.*, ed. Stephen Williams, 30–69. *Peabody Museum of Archaeology and Ethnology, Harvard University, Papers* 58.

———, and **Preston Holder**
1945 "A Prehistoric Ceremonial Complex in the Southeastern United States." *American Anthropologist* 47: 1–34.

Watson, V. D.
1950 "The Wulfing Plates." *Washington University Studies, Social and Philosophical Sciences* n.s. 18.

Webb, Clarence H.
1968 "The Extent and Content of Poverty Point Culture." *American Antiquity* 33 (3): 297–321.
1971 "Archaic and Poverty Point Zoomorphic Locust Beads." *American Antiquity* 30 (1): 105–114.
1977 "The Poverty Point Culture." *Geoscience and Man* 17.

Webb, William S.
1946 "Indian Knoll, Site Oh 2, Ohio County, Kentucky." *The University of Kentucky Reports in Anthropology and Archaeology* 4 (3): pt. 1.

———, and **Raymond Baby**
1957 *The Adena People No. 2.* Columbus: Ohio University Press.

———, and **W. Haag**
1940 "The Wright Mounds." *The University of Kentucky Reports in Anthropology and Archaeology* 5: 6–134.

———, and **Charles E. Snow**
1945 "The Adena People." *The University of Kentucky Reports in Anthropology and Archaeology* 6.

Welch, L. B., and J. M. Richardson
1881 "A Description of Prehistoric Relics Found near Wilmington, Ohio." *American Antiquarian and Oriental Journal* 4: 40–48.

West, G. A.
1932 "Tobacco, Pipes and Smoking Customs of the American Indians." *Milwaukee Public Museum Bulletin,* 17.

Willey, Gordon
1945 "The Weeden Island Culture: A Preliminary Definition." *American Antiquity* 10: 173–185.
1949a "Archaeology of the Florida Gulf Coast." *Smithsonian Institution, Miscellaneous Collections* 113.
1949b "Excavations in Southeast Florida." *Yale University Publications in Anthropology* 41.

Williams, Stephen, and John M. Goggin
1956 "The Long-nosed God Mask in the Eastern United States." *Missouri Archaeologist* 18 (3).

Willoughby, Charles C.
1932 "History and Symbolism of the Muskhogeans and the People of Etowah." *Etowah Papers*, 7–105. New Haven: Yale University Press.

———, and E. A. Hooton
1922 "The Turner Group of Earthworks, Hamilton County, Ohio." *Peabody Museum of American Archaeology and Ethnology, Harvard University, Papers* 8 (3).

Winters, Howard D.
1967 "An Archaeological Survey of the Wabash River in Illinois." *Illinois State Museum, Report of Investigations* 10.
1968 "Value Systems and Trade Cycles of the Late Archaic in the Midwest." In *New Perspectives in Archaeology*, ed. S. R. Binford and L. R. Binford, 175–222. Chicago: Aldine.
1969 "The Riverton Culture." *Illinois State Museum, Report of Investigations* 13.
1974 Introduction to William S. Webb, *Indian Knoll*. Reprint. Knoxville: The University of Tennessee Press.

———, and Nancy Hammerslough
1970 "The Havana Tradition." In *Adena: The Seeking of an Identity*, ed. B. K. Swartz, Jr., 138–141. Muncie: Ball State University.

Witthoft, John
1949 "Green Corn Ceremonialism in the Eastern Woodlands." *University of Michigan Museum of Anthropology, Occasional Contributions* 13.

238

PHOTO CREDITS

Photographs not taken by Dirk Bakker were generously provided by the following individuals and institutions: Ohio Historical Society, Columbus (figs. 5, 24, 28, 29); The National Museum of Natural History, Smithsonian Institution, Washington, D.C. (fig. 6); James A. Brown (figs. 17, 20, 22); The Museum of the American Indian, Heye Foundation, New York (figs. 19, 23); Field Museum of Natural History, Chicago (figs. 25, 27, 32); The Mound City Group National Monument, Chillicothe, Ohio (fig. 31); Hillel Burger, Peabody Museum photographer, Peabody Museum of Archaeology and Ethnology, Cambridge (copyright President and Fellows of Harvard College, 1984) (pls. 33, 36, 43, 45, 93, 122, 132); and the Georgia Department of Natural Resources, Parks and Historic Sites Division, Atlanta (pl. 69).